The Mystery Fancier

Volume 2 Number 6
November December 1978

THE MYSTERY FANCIER

Volume 2 Number 6
November/December 1978

TABLE OF CONTENTS

MYSTERIOUSLY SPEAKING. 1
Behind the Scenes at Bouchercon 9: Or, It Was Murder at
   the Bismarck! by Mary Ann Grochowski 3
Miss Marple She Isn't, by David H. Doerrer 7
Agatha Christie Is Still Alive and Well, by Amnon
   Kabatchnik 9
When Is This Stiff Dead? Detective Stories and Defini-
   tions of Death, by Thompson and Banks. 11
The Weevil in Beancurd: Or, The Cop Abroad, by
   George N. Dove 17
The Nero Wolfe Saga, Part X, by Guy M. Townsend. 20
IT'S ABOUT CRIME, by Marvin Lachman. 27
MYSTERY*FILE: Short Reviews by Steve Lewis 30
VERDICTS (More Reviews). 36
THE DOCUMENTS IN THE CASE (Letters). 43
Statement of Ownership 61

The MYSTERY FANcier
is edited and published bi-monthly by Guy M. Townsend,
1120 Bluebird Lane, Memphis, Tennessee 38116, U.S.A.
Contributions of all descriptions are welcomed. Deadline for the January/February 1979 issue: 15 December.

SUBSCRIPTION RATES: Domestic second class mail, $7.50 per year (6 is-
sues); Overseas surface mail, $7.50; Overseas airmail, $12.00. Overseas subscribers please pay in international money order, check drawn
on U. S. bank, or currency; no checks drawn of foreign banks, please.
Make checks payable to Guy M. Townsend, not *The MYSTERY FANcier*.

Second class postage paid at Memphis, Tennessee

Copyright 1978 by Guy M. Townsend
All rights reserved for contributors
ISSN:0146-3160

MYSTERIOUSLY SPEAKING . . .

SUBSCRIPTION RENEWALS

Except for a very few privileged characters, all subscriptions expire with this issue. Unless you contributed to one or more issues of volume two, you must pay the full subscription price to receive volume three. As previously announced, there has been a price increase. All domestic subscriptions are now $9.00 for six issues via second class mail. Overseas surface mail subscriptions are also $9.00, while Overseas airmail subscriptions remail $12.00. (Yes, Martha, I do lose money on overseas airmail subs, but I like to keep our foreign subbers current, and surface mail can take as much as three or four months, or even longer.)

TMF does not pay for contributions, except to give each contributor credit toward his next years subscription for each issue in which his material appears. Below is a list of contributors to volume two. The numbers in parentheses indicate the issues to which they contributed, and the dollar amounts indicate how much they must pay for a subscription to volume three.

Adey (2,3,4)	$4.50	Jobst (1)	$7.50
Albert (2,3)	6.00	Juri (1)	7.50
Bakerman (1,2,3,4,5)	1.50	Kabatchnik (1,4,5,6)	3.00
Balopole (1)	7.50	Kelley (1,2,4,5)	3.00
Banks (1-6)	0.00	Kutzner (5)	7.50
Bleiler (1,3,5)	4.50	Lachman (1-6)	0.00
Breen (1,3,5,6)	3.00	Lansdale (3,4,5,6)	3.00
Brincy (1,2,3,4,6)	1.50	Lewis (1-6)	0.00
Broecker (3)	7.50	McCahery (5)	7.50
Broset (1,2,3,5,6)	1.50	McCarthy (1)	7.50
Cramer (1)	7.50	McSherry (1)	7.50
Crider (4,5,6)	4.50	Masser (2)	7.50
Dillon (6)	7.50	Mertz (1,3,4,5)	3.00
Doerrer (2,3,4,6)	3.00	Meyerson (1-6)	0.00
Doran (2,4,5,6)	3.00	Moskowitz (5)	7.50
Dove (6)	7.50	Motsinger (6)	7.50
Dukeshire (3,4,5,6)	3.00	Nehr (3,4,6)	4.50
Fick (1)	7.50	Nevins (4,5)	6.00
Fiene (3)	7.50	Nieminski (5)	7.50
Frazier (1,4,6)	4.50	Parnell (5)	7.50
French (1,2,4)	4.50	Portser (3)	7.50
Goldman (4)	7.50	Pross (1,2,3)	4.50
Goldsmith (1)	7.50	Rall (1)	7.50
Goodrich (1)	7.50	Sandulo (2,3)	6.00
Gorman (2)	7.50	Seeger (6)	7.50
Grand (6)	7.50	Shibuk (1,2,4,5)	3.00
Grochowski (2,3,5,6)	3.00	Stilwell (2,3)	6.00
Hamilton (2,6)	6.00	Vicarel (2)	7.50
Hensley (4,6)	6.00	Waterhouse (1)	7.50
		Wooster (4,5,6)	4.50

No guarantees of complete accuracy on this, so if you're not on the list but should be, or if I've omitted an issue that you were in, just let me know. Remember, though, that letters that merely ask for aid or information do not count as contributions.

Once again I'd like to extend special thanks to those of

you who contributed most heavily; to Jeff Banks, Marv Lachman, Steve Lewis and Jeff Meyerson, who made every issue; and to Jane Bakerman, Bob Briney and Myrtis Broset who made every issue but one. And, what the hell, to Jon Breen, Dave Doerrer, Dave Doran, Ted Dukeshire, Mary An Grochowski, Amnon Kabatchnik, George Kelley, Joe Lansdale, Steve Mertz and Charlie Shibuk, who made four of the past six issues. These are the folks who have done the bulk of the work of making TMF volume two even better than volume one, and I appreciate it.

Before I forget it, there are a few books I want to mention--not to review, mind you, just to draw to your attention. First, E. F. Bleiler, who did such great things for our genre while he was at Dover (and who from time to time graces the pages of TMF with contributions) has had the new edition of his *Checklist of Science Fiction and Supernatural Fiction* published by Firebell Books in Glen Rock, NJ. It's hardbound, and well-bound at that, but I don't have a price on it. I mention it because Ev is one of us, because a number of the items in it do relate to our field, and because it is just a superb piece of work, capable of extracting praise even from the mouths (or pens or typewriters) of those, like myself, who do not care much for science fiction or supernatural fiction. Another TMF subber, who has yet to contribute, is Steven M. Krauzer who, with William Kittredge has edited and introduced an anthology entitled *The Great American Detective*, just published by Mentor Books (NAL) at $2.25. Some of the selections might raise an eyebrow here and there, but, what the hell, I'm probably just miffed because Steve didn't include the Rex Stout story I suggested to him. Penguin Books, God love 'em, continues to reissue old and not so old mysteries. The latest of Peter Lovesey's Victorian detective novels that they have released is *Swing, Swing Together*, at $1.95. Since this just happens to be the best historical detective series going, you might just want to pick this one up if you don't already have it. And Penguin has also reissued Erskine Childers' *Riddle of the Sands* ($1.95), which is almost worth buying for the fantastic cover alone, even if you already have the Dover reprint. Another one to keep an eye out for if you are an Agatha Christie fan is her *Autobiography*, which Ballantine has just released in paperback at $2.75.

One of these days I've just got to get organized. I have an item here left over from last March which I have forgotten to mention in every issue between then and now. I am told that there is a fanzine called *Cloak and Dagger* being put out by Jim Huang, 66 N. Virginia Ct., Englewood Cliffs, NJ 07632. That's all I know; I haven't even had time to write about a copy. Which brings something else to mind. Traditionally-- twice can be said to constitute a tradition--The Line-Up appears in the first issue of each volume. I have already said that I lack the time and the knowledge to do it for volume three and I have asked for a volunteer to undertake it. To date no one has come forward. If there is anyone who would like to tackle it at this late date, write to me immediately. I'm going to try to get back on schedule with the next issue (is there an echo in here?), so it will have to be quick.

Apologies for the poor repro on the last issue. I never did get an operator's manual for the offset press, so I had to wing it. (An apt expression, that, because operating an offset press without instructions is rather like having to land an aircraft after the pilot has had a heart attack.) I
(Continued on p. 35)

BEHIND THE SCENES AT BOUCHERCON 9
OR
IT WAS MURDER AT THE BISMARCK!

By Mary Ann Grochowski

> . . . Since you asked me to do a commentary on Bouchercon . . . I decided to submit to you a sort of tongue in cheek interpretation of the behind the scene fun. Since I didn't get to hear anything but snatches of the various talks, I could not, in any sincere vein, report on the panels, and I am sure Don Yates will do an admirable job. However, I thought your readers might like to get to know some of the participants a little more intimately. If you don't feel you want to publish the article, please don't feel you have to. Just don't call me the Rhona Barrett of Mysterydom!

It was with a good deal of trepidation that I and a friend set off in my trusty station wagon which was jammed to the ceiling with cartons of books to travel the 200 miles from Milwaukee to Chicago's Loop and the Bismarck Hotel, scene of the 1978 Bouchercon. Not only did I lack confidence in my ability to cope with the Loop traffic, but the disappointment of not being able to attend many of the scheduled discussions because of having committed myself to selling books at the convention was weighing heavily on my mind, almost as heavily as those 25 cartons of books were weighing down my car's rear axle. In addition, there was the added anxiety over the talk I was to deliver about Craig Rice on the panel regarding Chicago authors which had been assigned to me only a week before.

Accompanied by the friendly chatter of my companion, Patricia Guy, the trip passed very quickly, and we soon pulled up at the front of the hotel. An ominous reception greeted us there. From the askance looks directed at our cargo, we began to feel just a little unwelcome. After being directed to the delivery entrance, we were brusquely informed that no book room had been assigned to any group in the hotel. What's more, no one had heard of Bouchercon and we were even asked if we were sure we had the right hotel! Finally the understanding that there was a convention of mystery authors to be held at the Bismarck was established and my load of literature escorted to the Greenbriar room, located in the basement of the hotel.

Checking into our rooms was another adventure. Who said there is never a 13th floor in a hotel?? Much to our astonishment, we found ourselves inhabiting Room 1333 and the elevator which transported us there was inhabited by a ghostly female voice with a decided Southern accent, who mysteriously announced the direction of our travels and called out the numbers of the lower floors. It is extremely disconcerting when returning to your hotel room at 3:30 in the morning after an evening filled with mysterious discussion and the imbibing of great quantities to witch's brew to have the elevator doors close and a strange voice announce, in a seemingly empty elevator, "Goint up!" One other unusual mechanical gimmick standard in most rooms of the hotel was the ability to simultaneously turn on the lights and the television or radio, or all three. Many of the Bouchercon members suffered a severe shock when returning alone to a room shared with another person. Afterning on the light, they began to disrobe, and suddenly were confronted with the voice of an apparent stranger! It seems the TVs and radios took a short time to warm up, just long enough to take their unwary victims by surprise.

Five p.m. Friday found Patricia and me frantically unpacking our books in a small room off the main lecture room which the hotel personnel had assured us was the right place. Alphabetizing several hundred books is always an intriguing adventure, particularly when confined to the space of two rectangular tables. As a consequence, the announcement an hour later by the chairman of Bouchercon, Robert Hahn, that we were really supposed to be in a room upstairs somewhere was met with groans of dismay. Luckily, Bob was able to work things out with the hotel management so that we and all the other dealers were able to remain downstairs next to the lecture room, which was probably fortunate for all of the convention participants since business was decidedly good.

Some of the first visitors to the bookroom on Friday evening included Donald Yates, editor and translator of *Latin Blood*, an anthology of mystery stories written by Spanish speaking authors, a mystery author and college professor as well as an avid collector. His dark brown eyes lit up appreciably as he spotted two Gardner books which he needed for his collection. Cary Joseph Black, a serious Detroit collector, accompanied him.

Otto Penzler, author, editor, publisher and mystery critic, made the pleasant announcement of his plans to open a bookstore on Manhattan's West side devoted exclusively to the mystery genre and handling out of print, first editions, and a moderate selection of new books. He plans the grand opening for the early part of December 1978. Otto has also purchased the rights to publish *The Armchair Detective*, the foremost authoritative fanzine written about the mystery genre, edited by Allen Hubin.

Francis M. Nevins, Jr., lawyer, professor and author--Mike Nevins to serious mystery fans--arrived with Thelma Keeler, widow of Harry Stephen Keeler who was an amazing webwork author of the 30's and 40's. Mrs. Keeler discovered one of her husband's books which she did not have, and graciously offered to trade one of her duplicates for it. Mike Nevins gave a lecture about Harry Stephen Keeler early Saturday morning which was delightful, complete with maps of Keeler's universe and amusing anecdotes about Keeler's personal life. He revelaed that there are still about 25 unpublished manuscripts which Keeler left behind. The aftermath of Mike's superlative lecture was the complete deletion of the Keeler books from the book tables, as eager fans became Keeler converts.

Walter B. Gibson, alias Maxwell Grant, the guest of honor, author of The Shadow series, was on hand early Friday evening. A large, white-haired, convivial man, very young for his 81 years, Mr. Gibson entertained and intermingled with all of the mystery fans present on an informal basis, and was more than willing to autograph any Shadow memorabilia which the awed fans produced. One of the bookdealers, The Curious Bookshop, from East Lansing, Michigan, had a well-stocked supply of Shadow pulps, comic books, records, etc. Robert Weinberg, a dealer from Chicago, had a good supply of the recent Shadow paperbacks on hand, and delivered a very informative lecture on Sunday dealing with the history of the pulps.

Robert Fish, author of *Schlock Holmes, Kek Huuygen, Smuggler*, and numerous Jose De Silva novels was found to be an adept conversationalist, particularly by Sherlockians.

Chris Steinbrunner, co-author of *The Encyclopedia of Mystery and Detection* and film afficianado, though a late riser, was always on hand for the evening festivities, particularly the films, some of which were contributed by him.

J. Randolph Cox, mystery buff and foremost authority on Nick Carter, provided a silent movie about Nick Carter the detective, of course, and a very interesting commentary about the development of the Carter series, both in the pulp magazines as well as on film.

Guy Townsend, editor of *The MYSTERY FANcier*, graced the book room with his distinguished presence and the latest copies of TMF which were ready for subscribers to pick up. Guy is so professional and "together", although not at all strait-laced, that he could wear a bright checkered suit on Sunday and make it look conservative. He was also able to trade nostalgia, trivia, and puzzle questions with experts like Don Yates and John Nieminski for hours while consuming his fair share of brew! And would you believe that Guy and Martin Wooster were able to spend several hours together at a cocktail party Saturday evening, even sharing the same couch, without ever coming to blows!!

John Nieminski, editor of *Baker Street Miscellanea* and compiler of the *Ellery Queen Mystery Magazine* Index 1941 to 1973, is another trivia expert who had everyone straining to match his clever repartee.

John McAleer, author of *Rex Stout*, the biography which won an Edgar Award this year from the Mystery Writers of America, who is also a Ph.D. professor at Boston College, turned out to be a wonderfully informal, congenial man who entertained everyone with his stories about Stout which never appeared in the biography.

Jane S. Bakerman, associate professor of English literature at Indiana State University and author of numerous articles in mystery fanzines, is a soft spoken, very nice lady who obviously enjoys both mysteries and people.

Bob Briney, editor of the *Rohmer Review* and an expert on locked room mysteries was able to help clear up many puzzling conversations about who wrote what and what happened when.

Ellen Nehr, mystery fan par excellence, is a total delight. Although she hasn't been "provocative in at least ten years," or so she says, she sure did her best at provoking some scintillating and titillating conversation during the late evening and early morning cocktail parties.

A Manhattan resident, and owner of a cat named Lucretia, Mickey Fromkin was a joy to meet again. She has the unique habit of reading all of her unread books in chronological order. Reportedly, she is currently up to the year 1940. Talk about living in the past!

Mary Groff, author of many fascinating fanzine articles, left a sickbed to attend the conferences but was forced to return home to San Francisco on Saturday with a temperature of 104. We all hope she has fully recovered.

Al Nussbaum, the very congenial gentleman who turned from the vocation of bank robber to that of mystery writer with the help and encouragement of Dan Marlowe, helped to enliven many a cocktail party of discussion. Dan Marlowe was not present, but is currently residing with Al in California where he hopes to resume his writing career. Some of you probably know Dan suffered a stroke a while ago and lost all of his personal memory, including knowledge of all of his books. But, as fate would have it, Al was able to repay the debt of gratitude which he feels for Dan's helping him by this time helping Dan stage a writing comback.

James M. Ullman, author of several mystery novels and many short stories, a Chicago resident, was kept busy autographing books for fans. Percy Parker, another Chicago mystery author, was also present.

Dave Doerrer, collector and mystery buff, returned home to Florida penniless but happy with all of the wonderful finds he made in the bookroom.

A neighbor of Allen Hubin, Steve Stillwell, was very quick to show his expertise and made many new friends, particularly Guy Townsend, whose checkered jacket he ended up wearing.

Max Collins, writer of the Dick Tracy comic strip, and author of the Quarry series, breezed in on Sunday and was happy to greet again Bob Randisi who did the excellent interview of Max for volume 11, number 3 of *The Armchair Detective*. Bob Randisi, who also did the outstanding interview for TAD of Bill Pronzini, made the surprising revelation that the interview with Bill had been done by mail! According to Bob, who ought to know, Bill is currently hard at work on a new novel in Majorca.

The editor of DAPA-EM, an amateur fanzine which publishes collectively the fanzines of as many as 25 people, Art Scott, had a great time trading reminiscences with other members of DAPA-EM who were present and did a marvelous job of explaining DAPA-EM, which is certainly no ordinary publication, to other convention participants.

Jefferey Meyerson, illustrious editor of *The Poisoned Pen*, as warm and soft-spoken as his wife Jackie is warm and vivacious, was the host of one of the most well-attended cocktail parties on Saturday evening. Tall, with long hair and full beard, Jeff succeeds in looking scholarly, while Jackie, tall with long hair also, but lacking a beard, is absolutely effervescent. They did a fine job of making everyone feel at home.

Of course, there were many more wonderful people present, some of whom I never did get to meet. And I certainly regret not having been able to attend most of the formal panels, but the informal conversation was extremely informative and immensely gratifying. An engagement was announced, friendships were made and renewed, jobs were offered and confirmed, writing assignments were made and accepted, plots were hatched and rehashed. Conversations went on until even the mysterious voice in the elevator began to sound weary. The worst moments were trying to catch even a few hours of sleep knowing that somewhere within the depths of the hotel a party was still going on and wonderful gems of knowledge were being shared. Waking up at 7:00 a.m. was even more traumatic until a visit to the breakfast room revealed many more early risers who were just as eager to continue where the conversation had *(Continued on p. 8)*

MISS MARPLE SHE ISN'T

By David H. Doerrer

Intentionally humorous crime stories are a rather special sub-field of the genre, and I have found good ones more often the exception than the rule. While her efforts may not appeal to everyone, I would rate Joyce Porter among the more successful contemporary practitioners. Porter is probably best known for her series of novels featuring the obese, obnoxious Inspector Wilfred Dover and his long-suffering aide, Sergeant MacGregor. Were Dover to meet an untimely end in the course of one of his misadventures, his colleagues at Scotland Yard would be more likely to drop the case into the dead file at once than to work overtime to apprehend his murderer. To know this elephantine antithesis of Roger West and George Gideon is not, I am afraid, to love him.

Less well known, but more deserving of a sympathetic reception, is Porter's amateur feminine sleuth, the Honourable Constance Morrison-Burke, affectionately referred to as the "Hon Con". Blessed with inherited (and presumably tax-proof) wealth, cursed with a restless nature, occasionally canny yet more often incredibly naive, almost totally innocent of tact with the hide of a rhinoceros, the Hon Con made her debut in *Rather a Common Sort of Crime* (New York: McCall, 1970).

Infuriated by her dismissal as a volunteer with the Citizen's Advice Bureau of Totterbridge--a hapless client had taken the Hon Con's advice to chain herself to the Town Hall's railings to protest a plumbing problem--she sets up as a one-woman competitor. Her first--and only--customer has been rejected by her prudent and more orthodox rivals across the street. Rodney Burberry's mother wants someone to prove that her late son's indisputably voluntary ingestion of whiskey liberally laced with Kil'mkwick was murder and not--as the police have already decided--suicide. Such proof, she believes, will assure his soul's transfer to Heaven, not to mention putting a halt to her "friends" pious condolences.

Determined to best her erstwhile companions, the Hon Con agrees to "look into the case." This she proceeds to do by first extorting the official police reports from the hapless Detective-Sergeant Fenner. Despite misgivings upon learning what a nasty piece of business Rodney really was, the Hon Con, once committed, perseveres, ably albeit most reluctantly, aided by her companion, Miss Jones. An early clue to both the motive and the murderer's identity is fairly planted, and the Hon Con's efforts at detection are eventually, if unexpectedly, successful, although they are as bumbling as her manners are uncouth.

Fresh from her first "triumph", our heroine rises eagerly to the challenge of unmasking--preferably before the police--the killer of the lovely Teresa Eucharia Maria O'Coyne, a neighbor's au pair girl. Lacking a client in *A Meddler and Her Murder* (New York: McKay-Washburn, 1973), the Hon Con offers her services--à la Miss Marple--to the police as an invaluable source of local information. Unfortunately, her resemblance to the omniscient sage of St. Mary Mead ends with the fact that both are female. Her relations with her neighbors are so distant--where they are not actively hostile--that she is forced to spend most of this slower-moving tale painstakingly acquiring information already known to the police. She is even humiliatingly reduced to accepting much of it second-hand from the disapproving Miss Jones, who has listened in comfort to Mrs. Monday, the egg lady, while the Hon Con has endured cold, wind and rain in her house-to-house canvas.

Yet once again sheer determination wins out over utter incompetance. Slowly, and in some cases reluctantly, she eliminates the various suspects. On the very brink of admitting defeat, the Hon Con once again inadvertently stumbles upon a piece of information which points unmistakably to the murderer's identity. It is a hollow victory, however, for the police (and, I suspect, the reader) are well ahead of her this time.

The Hon Con's most recent opportunity[1] to exercise her rather dubious skills as a detective occurs during a group tour of the Soviet Union. In *The Package Included Murder* (Indianapolis: Bobbs-Merrill, 1976) no less than six attempts are made on the life of the luscious Penelope Clough-Cooper. Convincing her fellow travellers--even the endangered Penelope--that the last thing they want is to become embroiled with the Soviet police, the Hon Con, again accompanied by the martyred Miss Jones, sets out to solve the crime. Not until a murder does occur in the almost deserted airport upon the group's return to England does she understand the motive behind the earlier attempts. But better late than never, as the Hon Con herself might say, she does succeed in putting the police on the right track.

The misadventures of the Honourable Constance Morrison-Burke and Miss Jones do not and will not appeal to everyone, nor will they be remembered as great or even noteworthy contributions to mystery and detective fiction. Even their author has said "the books I write are meant to be wolfed down at one gulp on a train journey, or wherever, and thrown away. I don't expect anyone to read them half a dozen times . . . ."[2] Truly disparaging words from an author, and yet second-hand copies are not common on sales lists. Of course, this could simply be a reflection of small U.S. sales, but I'd like to think that it may also indicate that some readers have discovered that they like the Hon Con well enough not to discard the novels after a single reading. Don't read them for freshness of plot, for suspense or for action, but do try them if you appreciate, as I do, that very British humor which can so closely approach--but never becomes--slapstick.

---

[1] I have a reference to a 1977 (?) title, *Who the Heck is Sylvia?*, but have been unable to verify it.

[2] Joyce Porter, "The Solitary Life of the Writer", in *Murder Ink: The Mystery Reader's Companion,* perpetrated by Dilys Winn (New York: Workman, 1977), p. 82.

(continued from p. 6) ended only a few hours ago. To put it bluntly, it was murder at the Bismarck!

AGATHA CHRISTIE IS STILL ALIVE AND WELL

By Amnon Kabatchnik

Agatha Christie, who died two years ago at the age of 85, remains a phenomenon.

Her detective novels are still enormous best sellers in numerous languages, topped only by the Bible and the plays of Shakespeare. Her melodrama, "The Mousetrap", which opened in London twenty-six years ago, is still playing successfully, the longest running play in world theatre history. Following the stellar *Murder on the Orient Express* and *Death on the Nile*, additional motion pictures based on her stories are now planned.

A growing number of studies about Dame Agatha and her literary input have been published recently, testifying to her undiminished popularity.

H. R. F. Keating, crime critic for the London *Times* and author of the series of detective novels featuring Inspector Ghote of the Bombay C.I.D., has assembled some luminary practitioners in the field of suspense fiction, and they have put forward a combined look at *Agatha Christie: First Lady of Crime* (Holt, Rinehart and Winston, 224 pp., $12.95).

Elizabeth Walker, a distinguished writer of the supernatural, relates the Case of the Escalating Sales: Christie's first novel, *The Mysterious Affair at Styles* (1920) was rejected by several publishers, eventually accepted for publication, paying its author 125 dollars, selling a mere 2,000 copies. Gradually her books became increasingly popular, were translated into more than one hundred languages and to date their sales have exceeded 400 million copies.

Julian Symons, award winning author of crime novels, analyses Christie's works, concentrating mainly on her masterpieces *And Then There Were None*, *The Murder of Roger Ackroyd* and *The ABC Murders*. He theorizes that her chances of survival as an author who will be read a century from now are good, not because "she was a great or even a good writer" but "because she was the supreme mistress of a magical skill that is a permanent concern of humanity: the construction and the solution of puzzles."

Edmund Crispin, who has written eight detective stories which have secured his place in the annals of the genre, hails Agatha Christie's knack for simple plotting, solid construction, variety in her prose style and realism of English country life.

The anthology culminates with two portraits of Christie's most celebrated super-sleuths: Hercule Poirot, the eccentric Belgian with the egg-shaped head and waxed moustaches, whose "little gray cells" were the nemesis of clever criminals for over half a century; and Jane Marple, the tall, elderly spinster whose uncanny gift to fathom human nature was an important tool in her indefatigable investigative career.

The authors of two new books about the "Duchess of Death" are attempting to shed light on a factual baffling mystery--Agatha Christie's own notorious disappearance on Friday, December 3, 1926.

Gwen Robyns describes, in *The Mystery of Agatha Christie* (Doubleday, 247 pp., $8.95), the step-by-step occurances of the strange affair. The celebrated author did not return home that night. Her car, a green Morris, was found alongside a dirt road, the lights still on, its bodywork covered with hoarfrost.

On the seat of the car were a brown fur coat and a small dressing case which had burst open, scattering its contents of clothing and some papers, including an out-of-date driving license in the name of Mrs. Agatha Christie. There could be no doubt about the identity of the owner.

Agatha Christie's disappearance caused a sensation. Was she a victim of foul play? Did she commit suicide? Or was it an audacious publicity stunt? A nationwide search was immediately launched.

On the eleventh day of her absence, Agatha Christie was found under an assumed name, in an elegant hotel. It was proclaimed that she was suffering from loss of memory.

Gwen Robyns theorizes that in order to understand the bizarre disappearance it is important to learn that "it had been a traumatic year for Agatha Christie." Her mother had died after a severe illness, and her marriage to Colonel Archibald Christie had deteriorated drastically. He had become infatuated with a young woman.

Robyns then attempts to prove that Agatha Christie was more enigmatic than the puzzles she concocted. There are numerous tid-bits about Christie's aloofness from neighbors, readers and critics. She would grant interviews only on rare occasions, and had kept her financial matters under strict secrecy. But all that *The Mystery of Agatha Christie* manages to convey is a portrait of a shy, sensitive and recluse personality, with hardly an odd streak.

Robyns is more informative and interesting in the chapters dealing with Christie's contributions to the stage (notably "The Little Indians", "The Mousetrap", "Witness for the Prosecution" and "Spider's Web") and the silver screen (mainly the series of comedy-thrillers featuring Margaret Rutherford, the three versions of *And Then There Were None*, *Witness for the Prosecution* and *Murder on the Orient Express*).

There is also an amusing sequence about London's Detection Club, whose membership included Dorothy L. Sayers and G. K. Chesterton. The club's antics serve as ample proof that mystery writers are a unique breed.

Kathleen Tynan, the wife of critic Kenneth Tynan, has taken up the challenge of inventing an imaginary solution to the authentic disappearance of Agatha Christie, "a strange episode that had never been convincingly explained."

In *Agatha* (Ballantine Books, 247 pp. $2.95), Mrs. Christie is preoccupied with the painful realization that she is losing her husband to a younger rival. When he asks for a divorce she withdraws into herself--and disappears.

Tynan's speculative narrative attempts to penetrate the psyche of a woman betrayed. How will this accomplished mystery writer, so used to plotting intrigue and creating suspenseful incidents, react? Will she remain passive? Or will she direct her talents toward sinister revenge?

The events build up slowly to a surprising, shattering climax whose impact is not less effective than the last-minute revelations of Christie's better works.

Agatha Christie: First Lady of Crime, *The Mystery of Agatha Christie* and *Agatha* are respectable, affectionate epitaphs to one of the most popular authors of the century who may have passed away, but simply refuses to die.

WHEN IS THIS STIFF DEAD?
Detective Stories and Definitions of Death

By Leslie M. Thompson and R. Jeff Banks

While detective stories may represent only one genre of writing, they do seem to mirror to a great extent many of the attitudes of society at large. The various uses of violence in these stories certainly have counterparts in modern American society, and one could enumerate other parallels. One facet of this tendency, however, which has received little attention is the relationship between the ways in which detective stories define death and society's agonizing with this same problem. This paper, then, will investigate the various ways of defining death, and indicate the uses of these concepts in selected detective stories.

A person might assume that anyone knows how to define death, and certainly some detective stories and television programs imply the ease of defining death and isolating with pinpoint precision the time of its occurrence. Such, however, is not the case. Since the beginning of life itself, mankind has wrestled with the problem of defining or explaining not only life itself but its counterpart death. In fact, a traditional ploy has been to define one as the negation of the other. Thus, as late as 1821 J. G. Smith's *Principles of Forensic Medicine* boldly asserts:

> If we are aware of what indicates life, which everyone may be supposed to know, though perhaps no one can say that he truly and clearly understands what constitutes it, we at once arrive at the discrimination of death. It is the cessation of the phenomena with which we are so especially familiar--the phenomena of life.[1]

Obviously such non-definitions will not suffice in the world of modern medical technology, for matters relating to homicide, burial, transplantation, family relations, voting by proxy, and wills depend upon a precise notion of whether or not a person is dead or alive.

The discoveries of modern medical technology have compounded this problem of arriving at an exact definition of death, for any significant maans of preserving or prolonging life of necessity complicates the issue of death. Early humane societies in Europe and America, in fact, concerned themselves with early attempts to prolong life. In one of the society's lectures in 1790 Benjamin Waterhouse declared that "to blow in one's own breath into the lungs of another is an absurd and pernicious practice."[2] Two primary concerns influenced physicians of the time: 1) the fear of premature burial; and 2) an incipient awareness of the increasing legal, medical, and social complexity involved in defining death. The past hundred years have seen the diminution of the first of these worries and the exaggeration of the second, for while people may possibly still be buried alive or at least mistakenly designated as dead, this situation occurs only in the remotest of instances. Numerous studies attest to the fact that prior to this century a significant number of persons were buried while still alive, but modern machines such as the electrocardiogram and the electroencephalograph now minimize this possibility. On the other hand, modern life-saving devices greatly magnify the problem of ascertaining whether or not a person is technically or legally dead, for the same machines that save and sustain lives also make it possible to keep bodies alive even after they meet the technical definition of death.

An early attempt to come to grips with such situations can be seen in Ryan's profound statement in 1836 that "individuals who are apparently destroyed in a sudden manner, by certain wounds, diseases or even decapitation, are not really dead, but are only in conditions incompatible with the persistence of life."[3] Ryan, thus, recognizes the difference between somatic death, the extinction of the personality, and molecular death, the actual death of the cells which make up the body. This significant philosophical, ethical and legal point, however, will not likely mean a great deal to your average detective. One would hardly expect the following dialogue over the body of a person whose heart has been blown out:

"He's dead!"

"Naw, just in a state incompatible with the persistence of life."

So, while for the man on the street our poor victim is obviously dead, such generalization might not hold true in the courtroom with its far greater emphasis on the subtleties of law.

Even our detective, however, might need to know if the victim is indeed dead, and confirmation might be gained from one of the modern sets of criteria which would include: 1) total lack of response to external stimuli; 2) absence of spontaneous muscular movements, especially breathing; 3) absence of all reflexes; 4) total collapse of arterial blood pressure; 5) flat electrocardiogram; 6) flat electroencephalograph tracings. In some instances--especially those involving certain barbituates--even these criteria will not definitely prove death. Of course, most victims in detective stories usually obligingly die at least sooner or later, so that the plot can get down to the business of tracking down the killer. Accordingly, the average detective does not have to worry about Joseph Still's further elaboration that determining death should include the following five levels: 1) cellu-vegetative death; 2) organ death; 3) organismal death (heart and lungs stop); 4) psychic death; 5) vegetative death.

God forbid that the poor overburdened detective would even further be obligated to consider such factors as social death, spiritual death, and vegetative or metabolic death where machines keep organs and cells alive. Even more perplexing cases involve situations in research laboratories where scientists will keep alive for many years cells from otherwise deceased persons. To complicate the issue, cryonics (the freezing of bodies) promises the hope of resurrection at some future time when medical technology would be able to remedy the current cause of death. Perhaps this situation would give new meaning to the cliche that "Joe is in the deep freeze."

Some philosophers, doctors, and other researchers now consider death a disease which like a sickness can be cured. Just as some diseases remain beyond control, so too do some levels of death, but the terminology of disease applies; i.e.

"What happened to Harry?"

"He had an attack of death."

"Is he slightly dead?"

"No, he is very seriously dead."

While this discussion might seem remote to the plot of

most if not all detective stories, surprisingly these works deal directly and indirectly with various aspects of this topic. Indeed, definitions of death often serve as basic plot devices and legal, medical and social aspects of death also crop up frequently. News of death triggers either the reader's or the detective's interest in very nearly all murder mysteries: it's the source of the name.[4] Some stories also include the older mistaken notion that someone died at precisely 4:59 p.m. or other inaccurate assumptions about the nature and concept of death.

Fixing time of death with precision--though seldom is the "reader" informed just how such determination is achieved--is almost always significant, whenever a writer uses it, to the breaking of alibis and establishment of opportunity to have committed the crime. Typical examples of this occur in such books as *Give 'Em the Ax* by A. A. Fair (Gardner), p. 90 ff.; *No Business for a Lady* by J. L. Rubel, p. 111; *Michael Shayne's Long Chance*, p. 64, and *This Is It, Michael Shayne*, the latter two by Brett Halliday (Dresser).[5] Also typical were the Ellery Queen radio broadcasts, "The Adventure of the Singing Rat" (Jan. 7, 1943) and "The Adventure of the Scarecrow and the Snowman" (Jan. 20, 1944), as well as the Nero Wolfe radio episode "The Case of the Careless Cleaner" (Nov. 17. 1950).

We believe that similar uses of relatively precise times of death are to be found in at least one each 1940s film featuring Queen, Shayne (as played by Lloyd Noland, or at least in a film with Noland as the detective hero and released contemporaneously with his Shayne films) and Boston Blackie, as well as in other B-movie detective programs of the 1930s and '40s, but unfortunately we had no opportunity to test this belief in time for inclusion in this paper. It is also likely that early TV series, such as the first or second *Ellery Queen*, *Man Against Crime* and *Martin Kane, Private Eye*, had similar episodes, but those 1950s shows are truly inaccessible.

It is certain that the most recent TV *Queen* began with a pilot in which the time of death was fixed precisely and that the precision was essential to the detective's brilliant solution.[6] Even more recently, *Quincy* for Oct. 14, 1977, "A Question of Time", spent 40 minutes of Irving Perlberg's 51-minute script in Dr. Quincy's successful attempt to precisely fix the victim's time of death. In this case, not only apprehension (and, one hopes, the eventual punishment) of the guilty, but a large insurance claim and even continued profitable operation of the business where the death occured, hung upon "a question of time."[7]

With so many women detectives, writers and readers, it probably should follow that death has more often than not been treated with what might be termed an extremely feminine tendency to suppress the details, especially in older works. Mary Roberts Rinehart should have provided an early exception to this with her Nurse Adams books which could, and sometimes did, take the reader to the victim's deathbed. Here is the nurse's report, hardly a model of cool, professional detachment, from *Miss Pinkerton*. Note that the medical man's definition of death here probably differs little from the already cited one of J. G. Smith offered more than a century earlier.

> I ran back, to see miss Juliet in a convulsion on the bed.
> Over and over I have lived again those next few minutes. I have dreamed about them. In these dreams I am once again beside

the big walnut bed, with Doctor Stewart across from me and star-down at the old lady, and she is having that convulsion, jerking and twitching, and on her unconscious face that dreadful *risus sardonicus*, the sardonic mask which almost at once began to fade into the mask of death.

How long that lasted I do not know. *Time means nothing* in such a situation [emphasis added]. As the grin began to fade I remember that I glanced up at the doctor, and at that instant she gave a final convulsive shiver and then relaxed.

The doctor stared at her, and then straightened and looked across the bed at me.

"She is dead!"[8]

As little later as 1960, Ellis Peters' isolated houseparty in *Where There's a Will*--a reworking of Dame Agatha's *Ten Little Indians*--does considerably better at facing and describing death. The death scene begins fairly late in Chapter 4 and continues into Chapter 5, where the following is to be found.

The air was full of questions, upstairs and down, spoken and unspoken, and no one was answering them. The doctor swung a chair from the next table and sat down beside the old man's body, clasped the thin wrist for a moment, and stiffened perceptibly at the feel of the chilling skin under his fingers.

"Give me some more light, Neil, and get out of my way." He bent over the body, tilting the head gently back upon his arm, and the half-veiled eyes stared unmoved into the glare of the lamps.

. . .

No one spoke until the doctor lowered the heavy head gently, and pressed down the half-raised eyelids.

"Dead?" said Neil in a whisper.

"Quite dead. Been dead round about half an hour, I should judge."[9]

More recent writers have offered what we may term a more true-to-life approach. John Ball's Virgil Tibbs solved the mystery in his first book with a sensible observation that tissue degeneration following organismal death--naturally enough not using this terminology--proceeds more rapidly *In the Heat of the* [Deep Southern setting] *Night*. Tibbs' appearance on the scene where the body of a badly-decomposed murder victim has been discovered in his most recent adventure adds still another touch of modernity.

Virgil took off his coat and tie, hung them on a convenient bush, and tied a clean handkerchief over his face. These things done, he pulled a pair of rubber gloves over his dark hands and got down on his knees beside the body.

It was not agreeable work, but the job of a homicide specialist seldom is. The normal first consideration, whether or not life was extinct, did not even arise.[10]

In *The Death of the Detective* by Mark Smith, the triggering death, so far as the title character is concerned, is actually the second of a multitude in this involved and murky novel. The death of detective Magnuson's client occurs very significantly "just moments before" a first interview which should have dispelled much of the following mystery. Similarly untimely deaths abound in detective fiction, of course, the already cited *This Is It, Michael Shayne* providing one excellent example. What is of more interest to us here is the brief discussion of how his doctor established the client's death, in Chapter 21, followed by the victim's lawyer's reflection upon this news coupled with that of the existence of a new will.

Chandler dropped into the chair next to Magnuson and slapped his thighs with his palms. The mystery of this affair, once unravelled, would resolve itself not in high tragedy but comic opera. Legally a man should be considered dead when his mind was dead. He had a vision of Farquarson, in his final moments, turning to the solace of some primitive, mystical, faith-healing, holy-rolling religion that promised him, by his faith alone, salvation from brutal Hell. You could never be certain when the hellfire of crazed Presbyterians was in the blood, and you could never be certain with Frazer Farquarson in particular.[11]

Near the end of the book, the narrator underscores lawyer Chandler's "comic opera" judgment by remarking:

Legal battles over the estate can be expected for years to come. Mainly because the coroners and medical experts have given as the times of death of Farquarson, Bonny Wenzel, and Al Wenzel a range of hours that overlap each other, making it possible, in theory anyway, that any one of them could have died before the other. Which means that if Farquarson were still alive at the time of Bonny Wenzel's death, those same distant Farquarson relatives who are challenging Cavan's share of the estate will inherit her share. Therefore the battle taking place is not only between the Farquarson relatives, but between the Fraquarson relatives and Bonny Wenzel's heirs, with Cavan who had originally been presumed the principal Farquarson heir left on the sidelines watching the fray.[12]

This statement brings us almost back to our starting point and thus we find in detective stories the same kind of misconceptions and uncertainties about death that characterize attitudes in the general public. In both areas, however, we find a slow progression toward a fuller understanding of the complexities of this problem, but neither the general public nor the world of detective fiction yet evidences great likelihood of soon coming to full grips with the implications of this situation.

NOTES

[1] David Hendin, *Death as a Fact of Life* (New York, 1973), p. 17.

[2] *Ibid.*, p. 18.

[3] Keith Mant, "The Medical Definition of Death," in *Death: Current Perspectives*, ed. by Edwin S. Shneidman (Palo Alto, CA., 1976), p. 225.

[4] Exceptions, such as the blackmail investigation in *The Big Sleep* (Chandler), the "red herring" mate-watching in *Chinatown* (film) and the kidnapping in *The Twisted Thing* (Spillane), are clever and infrequent (surely well below 5% of the total) variations of formula. Ross Macdonald's studious avoidance of the standard opening represents a new, and largely personal, formula, which may help explain his great celebrity. Another new formula opening has appeared in the police procedural subgenre, where frequently a spate of lesser crimes (often at least partly ludicrous with humorous intent) are considered first, by reader and detective alike, building up the the murder as a climactic crime—sometimes quite late in the book. This might well be called the *Adam-12* formula, although more often than not the climactic crime on episodes of that TV series was not murder. We have been unable to find any writer of a substantial number of procedurals who uses "the *Adam-12* formula" exclusively, but some certainly do so extensively.

[5] As readers will be well aware, Gardner's adventure of Donald Lam and Bertha Cool was published in many editions by William Morrow and Pocket

Books. Our citation is to the Armed Services Edition of 1945. The Rubel book was published by Gold Medal, 2nd printing, 1958. The two Mike Shaynes have also been issued several times by Dodd, Mead and by Dell; the editions cited are April 1961 and November 1962, respectively.

[6]This telefilm, starring Jim Hutton and David Wayne (as the Queens), Ray Milland, Kim Hunter and Monte Markham, was written by Richard Levinson and William Link. It was first broadcast March 22, 1975, as an NBC-TV *Sunday Mystery Movie*.

[7]Besides Jack Klugman (in the title role) and other regulars, the cast included Brenda Scott, Rudi Solari, Michael Lane, Irene Tedro and Peter Mark Richman.

[8]Mary Roberts Rinehart, *Miss Pinkerton* (New Dell Edition, May 1964), p. 141. Those who find access easier to some other edition will find we have quoted from the closing paragraphs of Chapter 18.

[9]Ellis Peters, *The Will and the Deed* (Avon, 1966), p. 49.

[10]John Ball, *The Eyes of Buddha* (Little, Brown, 1976), p. 7.

[11]Mark Smith, *The Death of the Detective* (Avon, 1975), p. 336.

[12]*Ibid.*, p. 611.

(Continued from p. 19) genre." Faithfullness to reality, says Waugh, demands that the hero of the procedural story be human rather than super-human, as do the restrictions of the policeman's job and the society he is sworn to uphold.
 Actually, I think we can go a step further than that. It is not just the demand for "realism" that keeps the police procedural low-key. I doubt if the lives of real police detectives are all that much less exciting than those of private detectives or, for that matter, secret agents. It is rather that the conventions of popular fiction have determined that private eyes be knights-errant and that spies be lonely individualists. As for the fictional policeman, he keeps on being a cop, whether in the home precincts of Stockholm or Amsterdam or in the more exotic environments of Budapest or Kyoto.

(Continued from p. 29) yard.
 Dan J. Marlowe and Al Nussbaum tell how the former helped the latter to go from bank robber to writer. In their articles, Donald Westlake and Christiana Brand are, naturally, humorous and delightful, respectively. In the best article, Richard Martin Stern goes back almost fifty years to recall a brutal kidnapping in his neighborhood. It is the high-spot of a generous, highly recommended anthology.

THE WEEVIL IN BEANCURD
Or, The Cop Abroad

By George N. Dove

In terms of setting and subject matter, the police procedural (sometimes called the police routine story) is the most recent development in detective fiction. It is also the most prosaic, lacking the intellectual glamor of the classic formal-problem story and the exotic sensationalism of the hard-boiled private investigator story. It got off to an unpromising start: aside from the pioneer efforts of Lawrence Treat and Hillary Waugh in this country and of Maurice Procter in England, writers did not take much interest in the procedural format until the enormous popularity of the "Dragnet" radio and TV series spawned a whole new crop of police stories in print, but even so no police procedural ever attained the popularity of the mystery novels of Agatha Christie or Ross Macdonald. As a matter of fact, ti was not until the publication of Dorothy Uhnak's *The Investigation* in 1977 that a single police procedural ever made the best-seller lists.

One reason for the absence of sensationalism in the police procedural is that the writers have generally preferred to keep the stories low-key, drawing their series characters from the ranks of ordinary hard-working police detectives instead of mental giants like Sherlock Holmes or knights-errant like Philip Marlowe. This preference on the part of the writers suggests an interesting question: Is the low-key approach in the police procedural an inherent part of the formula for this type of story, or is it an effort at "realism," consistent with the prosaic environments of ordinary crime and commonplace police work? One way of finding an answer to this broad question would be to state it more specifically: Suppose we take the police detective out of his customary surroundings and send him on a mission into a foreign country, where the excitement of the chase is heightened by a more exotic atmosphere than the one to which he is accustomed. Does our fictional policeman thereupon assume the role of a glamorous secret agent like Fleming's James Bond, or does he remain a cop, with a cop's attitudes and reactions?

The answer, as I will try to show in a brief analysis of three stories, is that he remains a cop, subject to much the same kinds of danger as he would have been back home, dealing with the same kinds of grubby criminals, reacting in the same matter-of-fact way to the provocations of sex, and maintaining his professional stance in regard to police work and espionage.

The first book is *The Man Who Went Up in Smoke* (1966), one of the Martin Beck series by Maj Sjöwall and Per Wahlöö. In this story Beck, of the Swedish National Police, finds it necessary to spend some time in Budapest in search of a missing person. The temptation to turn the novel into a sensational spy story at the height of the popularity of James Bond must have been exceptionally strong, as evidenced by two references to Bond early in the story, but the authors resisted. Beck does not attempt to maintain a cover, and he is considerably assisted in his task by the cooperation of a competent Hungarian policeman.

The second story is Nicolas Freeling's *The Lovely Ladies* (1971), in which Inspector Van der Valk of the Amsterdam Criminal Brigade goes to Dublin in search of a murder suspect. Like Martin Beck, Van der Valk works openly as a policeman without cover, and he shares Beck's advantage of cooperation by the Irish police.

The third one, Janwillem van de Wetering's *The Japanese Corpse* (1977), has all the accoutrements of a slam-bang tale of international intrigue: the aged (and un-named) commisaris and Sergeant De Gier of the Amsterdam police journey to Japan to assist in stopping the flow of stolen temple treasures and drugs to Europe, they maintain an elaborately established cover, and they work with an agent of the Japanese Secret Service. Van de Wetering, however, also declines the gambit of turning his police procedural into a sensational spy novel I will not spoil this fine story by giving away the ending, but the author's resistance to temptation is clearly evident in a tremendous build-up involving commando teams with bristling bayonets, followed by a resolution that is as prosaic and ludicrous as any in mystery fiction.

The contrast between the approach of the policeman and that of the secret agent comes through especially strongly in *The Japanese Corpse* when the agent who is working with the Dutch cops explains why he gave up police work:

I spent a year in the police before I joined the Service. Police methods are slow and boring, I thought. There are so many safeguards protecting the suspect that the investigating officer feels like a weevil in a bowl filled with beancurd.

Whatever else the cop abroad is, James Bond he is not. In all three of the stories the policemen are subjected to physical violence, but the attacks never involve such picturesque weapons as poisonous centipedes, tarantulas, or even high-powered rifles. Martin Beck is beaten up on a bridge in downtown Budapest, Van der Valk gets slugged on a street in Dublin and suffers a fractured collarbone, and a group of Japanese toughs come after the commisaris and De Gier with pistols and a shotgun. Each of the attacks could have happened in Stockholm or Amsterdam.

If the cop abroad is not James Bond, neither are his opponents Dr. No or Ernst Blofeld. The attackers of Martin Beck are a group of shabby drug-pushers, and the man who slugs Van der Valk is a tough with IRA connections. The fearsome daimyo, head of the Japanese gangsters, turns out to be a chubby fellow in his late sixties who reminds De Gier of a fat Chinese god.

Even the sex scenes have a ludicrously commonplace quality. Martin Beck unintentionally arouses the passion of a young woman who slips into his hotel room and proceeds to pull her dress over her head, but Beck's response is a stern "Please dress yourself," as it would have been when he was with the Public Morals Squad back in Stockholm. Van der Valk is also visited by a woman in his room, but even as he starts to make love to her on his rumpled bed his concern is for his fractured collarbone. De Gier makes love to a Japanese girl at a time when the gangsters are in the vicinity, and he can't help wondering how it would feel to get a bullet in the back of his neck at the moment of sexual climax.

Not only have the writers of these three books kept their narrative situations low-key; they also endow their cops abroad with typical policemen's attitudes toward the methods of foreign police, toward the game of espionage, and toward themselves as members of a world-wide profession.

Being professionals, the policemen naturally size up their foreign counterparts and compare them with their own organizations. Martin Beck admires the efficiency of the Hungarian police, though his democratic Swedish soul is a little offended by their authoritarianism. Van der Valk is positively envious of the way the Irish cops can organize an operation, telling himself that if he tried the same thing at home he would have to go through ten different government departments and wind up being sabotaged by petty departmental jealousies.

As policemen used to working in the open, they take a cynical view of international intrigue and covert activity. When Martin Beck is told that he can't be given any information about the mission until he has been briefed by the Foreign Office, he asks, "Have we started taking orders from them too?" De Gier and the commisaris consider secret service activity rather absurd. The commisaris is amused at the vision of himself waving a machine pistol and confides to De Gier that he had always wanted an opportunity to say, "I'll pump you full of lead." A little later, when the Japanese agent outlines a plan for storming the gangsters' stronghold with commando units, De Gier innocently asks, "Why can't we just have them arrested by the local police?"

They tend, rather, to identify with their opposite numbers on the regular foreign police forces and to reflect that cops are pretty much the same the world over. As Van der Valk looks at the tall, thin figure of Detective Inspector Flynn of the Dublin police and contemplates his countrified facial expression, he reflects on the fact that there is almost no other profession in which looking intelligent is such a disadvantage. Martin Beck gets off on the wrong foot with the Budapest police because he failed to check in with them on arrival, and he is soon accosted by Officer Szluka who announces coldly, "I'm from the police." "So am I," Beck replies. The two cops spar and parry with each other for a while, soon become collaborators and personal friends, and when Beck is attacked by the hoodlums, Szluka and his men intervene in time to prevent serious injury.

If the cop abroad remains a weevil in beancurd, he has nobody to blame but his chronicler. Sjöwall and Wahlöö could easily have let Martin Beck burn up the Hungarian highways in an Aston Martin (after all, operations behind the Iron Curtain never deterred James Bond), and van de Wetering could just as plausibly have put his Dutch cops up against a transcendent evil Japanese genius instead of an elderly slob. The consistent refusal of these writers to sensationalize their stories is a re-affirmation of the basic premise of the police procedural, in which the detective-protagonist is a human being of no remarkable attributes except his own professional competence, conscious of his own limitations and those of his job, shunning heroics and high drama.

What we are talking about, of course, is the pervasiveness of formula in popular fiction. Given the assumptions of the police procedural, the writer tends to follow the conventions of the craft even when the current tastes of the reading public may be running in another direction.

Hillary Waugh makes the important point that the writer of this kind of story is immediately in trouble, because "the attractive superman hero is denied him by the nature of the *(Continued on p. 16)*

THE NERO WOLFE SAGA
Part X

By Guy M. Townsend

"Too Many Detectives" [early 1956], published in *Three for the Chair*, 1957.

THE STORY ::: Wire-tapping scandals in New York, some involving private detectives, lead the New York Secretary of State to the startling discovery that the 590 licensed private detectives in New York state (432 in New York City alone) "took no written examination and no formal inquiry was made into their backgrounds." Furthermore, since the operatives employed by licensed detectives were not required to be licensed, there was no way even of telling how many people were employed in the detecting business in New York, much less regulating their activities effectively. In an effort to get a handle on this problem, the Secretary of State summoned all 590 licensed detectives to appear for questioning either in New York or in Albany. That Wolfe and Archie are summoned to Albany does nothing to improve Wolfe's opinion of the whole operation, nor does the fact that the only wiretapping activity in which he ever engaged turned out to be a source of gross embarrassment to him, as he had been tricked into operating an illegal tap by a man whith whom he never caught up afterwards. Arriving at the appointed place in Albany, Wolfe and Archie find five other New York City private detectives already present. Things become quite sticky when, after Wolfe, with considerable distaste, relates to the special deputy secretary of state his sole experience with wiretapping, the very man who had tricked Wolfe into doing the tap turns up dead in a room down the hall from where Archie, Wolfe and the other detectives had been waiting. An officious Albany chief of detectives arrests Wolfe and Archie as material witnesses. Though they get out on bail, they can't leave the city of Albany, so Wolfe solves the murder so that he can go home. It's really quit e obvious who the murderer has to be (so why didn't I tumble to it until after Wolfe explains all?).

WOLFE ::: Wolfe takes his being made a fool of very seriously: "'I had been flummoxed.' Wolfe swallowed hard. 'Utterly flummoxed,' he said bitterly." "The silliest blunder I have ever made has found me here today, to my deep chagrin and possibly my undoing." Several times he speaks of the "ignominy" of his situation. Before the body is discovered Wolfe remarks, "For a month most of Mr. Goodwin's time, for which I pay, was spent trying to find him, and Mr. Goodwin is a highly competent and ingenious man. . . . But he has by no means forgotten that client and neither have I. We never will." Wolfe and Archie spend four hours in jail before Park er manages through a colleague to spring them: "Of course I had been behind bars before, but never together with Wolfe. For him it was a first, since I had known him." Wolfe refuses to eat anything during the period of their incarceration. Several of Wolfe's habits and idiocyncracies are in evidence. Archie and Wolfe journey to Albany by car, with Wolfe "in the back seat of the sedan as usual so he wouldn't go through the windshield when we crashed." Wolfe says, "I don't carry a watch"; of course, he did wear one on his wrist in *In the Best Families,* and I seem to recall a pocket watch popping up before, but apparantly he had abandoned timepieces by this point in his life. "Though Wolfe never talks business at the table, he likes to talk while eating, about anything and everything but business, and nearly always does." Of Wolfe and women: "Sometimes he honestly tries to speak to a woman without frowning at her, but he seldom makes it." This time he does, however, and the lookee is Dol Bonner, about whom more later. When Wolfe starts thinking, Archie tells some others who are present "not to bother to keep their voices lowered, since nothing going on outside his head could disturb Wolfe when he was concentrating on the inside." A few other items: "Wolfe had his legs crossed, as usual when he was on a chair too small for him, and without arms"; Wolfe goes to bed with the hotel window wide open in the dead of winter, to the considerable discomfort of Archie, with whom he is sharing the room (*nota bene,* then see Wolfe's reaction to sharing a room with anyone in the next episode); and Wolfe wears a "dressing gown, a yellow wool number with fine black stripes." Finally, Wolfe shuts Archie out on this one, under circumstances which annoy Archie greatly.

ARCHIE ::: Archie on women in the profession:

I am against female detectives on principle. It's not always and everywhere a tough game, but most of the time it is, with no room for the friendly feelings and the nice little impulses. So a she-dick must have a good thick hide, which is not a skin I'd love to touch; if she hasn't, she is apt to melt just when a cold eye and hard nerves are called for, and in that case she doesn't belong. However, there are times when a principle should take a nap.

Archie regards the drinking of rum and coke as a "flaw". He drinks milk in this one--"I like a drink occasionally, but not when I'm out on bail. Then I need all my faculties." Wolfe's characterization of Archie as "a highly competent and ingenious man" has already been mentioned. Wolfe also remarks: "he thinks it necessary to badger me into earning fees by taking jobs, which I would prefer to reject. I confess that he is sometimes justified." Finally, Wolfe says that Archie "claims that he never allows his watch to be more than thirty seconds off."

OTHER REGULARS ::: Fritz is mentioned a few times but, since all the action occurs in Albany, does not actually appear. Archie says that Fritz "suspects every woman who ever crosses the threshold of wanting to take over his kitchen, not to mention the rest of the house." Lon Cohen is spoken to over the phone, as is Nathaniel Parker (Parker's phone number is given as Eastwood 6-2605 this time). Saul--"the best there is"--plays a small part. Jay Kerr, Steve Amsel and Harland Ide are New York detectives who are involved in this episode. (Harland Ide's agency is mentioned in the following episode.) "Larry" Bascom is mentioned--is this Del Bascom? And then there's Dol Bonner: "Theodolinda (Dol) Bonner, about my age, with home-grown long black lashes making a curling canopy for her caramel-colored eyes, had had her own agency as a licensed detective for some years and was doing all right. . . . I had seen her before." From this last sentence, and from their relations during this episode, it seems likely that Dol and Archie and Wolfe had not been closely associated before.

PHYSICAL ASPECTS and ROUTINE AT THE BROWNSTONE ::: The automobile used in this episode is referred to simply as "the

sedan", no make or model specified. And that's it.
     ODDS & ENDS ::: Archie and Wolfe are both members of
ALPDNYS, the Association of Licensed Private Detectives of
New York State. It was on 5 April 1955 that a man calling
himself Otis Ross came to the brownstone and requested a tap
on the phone in "his" apartment on West 83rd St., thus beginning Wolfe's first and last phone-tapping enterprise.

Might As Well Be Dead [April 1956], published in 1956. WARN-
ING--a plot development is discussed in this section.
     THE STORY ::: Eleven years before, rich Omaha hardware
tycoon James R. Herold accused his son Paul of stealing
$26,000 and kicked him out. A month ago, however, Herold
discoverd that his son had indeed been innocent of the crime,
and the unrepentant bastard has graciously decided to take
his son back. Trouble is, young Paul has not been heard from
for eleven years except for some birthday cards to his mother
and sister postmarked New York. Herold's inquiries through
Lt. Murphy of Missing Persons fail to bear fruit, and on Murphy's recommendation Herold comes to Wolfe: "He said that on
a job like finding a missing person you yourself wouldn't be
much because you were too fat and lazy, but that you had two
men, one named Archie Goodwin and one named Saul Panzer, who
were tops for that kind of work." Neither Wolfe nor Archie
think much of Murphy's siccing Herold on them with a job Murphy clearly hopes they will fall flat on their faces with,
but Wolfe does agree to try to find the lost son. A "come
home, all is forgiven"-type ad in the newspaper addressed to
"P.H."--on the assumption that while Paul Herold probably
changed his name, he may well have retained the same initials
--has some unexpected results, one of which being to arouse
the suspicion and curiosity of the lawyer for Pete Hays, who
is on trial for the murder of the husband of the woman with
whom he is in love. Hays denies being Paul Herold, but won't
give any details about his early life. Wolfe straightens all
the tangles out--with even more than the customary bending of
the law--but three more people die before the real murderer
is apprehended. This episode is of especial interest in that
in it one of the regular characters is killed in the line of
duty--John Joseph ("Johnny") Keems.
     WOLFE ::: Another embarrassment of riches about Wolfe.
Well, here goes . . . . "For half an hour after lunch he
never gets above a mutter unless he has to." However, "Wolfe
can bellow." "One man who had made 'contact' a verb in that
office had paid an extra thousand bucks for the privilege,
though he hadn't known it." "He was working on a crossword
puzzle by Ximenes in the London *Observer*." "Wolfe is not a
handshaker." "When Wolfe sees that a point has to be conced-
ed he manages not to be grumpy about it." "He laughed. A
stranger would have called it a snort, but I know his different snorts." Here's the first mention of Wolfe's phonophobia:
"Except in emergencies the boys never call between nine and
eleven in the morning or four and six in the afternoon, when
he is up in the plant rooms, but even so the damn phone rings
when he's deep in a book or working a crossword or busy in
the kitchen with Fritz, and he hates it." "Wolfe, who rarely
turns in before midnight, was at his desk, reading *A Secret
Understanding* by Merle Miller." "Wolfe wants people at eye
level." "Mr. Wolfe is a genius, but geniuses have their weak
spots, and one of his is that he pretends to believe that attractive young women can refuse me nothing. It comes in

handy when an attractive young woman says no to something he wants, because it's an excuse for passing the buck to me." "From that room he has walked out on a lot of different people, but when a woman goes to pieces he doesn't walk out, he runs." "There were very few men whose tongues he had ever been willing to rely on [to keep a secret], and no women at all." Wolfe--"The more you put in a brain, the more it will hold--if you have one." "He pinched his nose. He has an idea that pinching his nose makes his sense of smell keener." When a woman says she and her husband sleep in the same room "Wolfe started to make a face, realized he was doing it, and called it off. The idea of sleeping in the same room with anybody on earth, man or woman, was too much." However, as we have seen, he made no fuss about sharing a hotel room with Archie in the previous story. He calls Joan of Arc "an inspired hoyden", which is generous. Archie "relieve[s] Fritz of the chore of taking Wolfe's breakfast tray up to his room, where, a mountain of yellow silk pajamas, he stood barefoot in the flood of sunshine near a window." "He hates to stand up right after a meal, and he hates to sit down in the kitchen because the stools and chairs aren't fit to sit on--for him." But in an earlier episode Archie says the kitchen was the only place that Wolfe didn't mind inadequate seating arrangements. "The thought of a hungry human, even a hungry murder suspect, even a hungry woman, in his house, is intolerable." Wolfe says "I never discuss business at the table", but elsewhere in this tale he all but orders Archie to deliver a piece of information relative to the case at hand, and he does it during dinner. "It was," Archie says, "a tough day for rules. Still another got a dent when, the dessert having been disposed of, we went to the office for coffee, but that happens fairly often." "When Wolfe gets desperate he is absolutely fearless. He will expose me to the risk of a five year stretch up the river without batting an eye." Finally, Wolfe says "Prudence is no shame to valor."

ARCHIE ::: Wolfe calls Archie "my confidential assistant", and elsewhere he remarks, "You have your gifts, Archie. I have always admired your resourcefulness when faced by barriers." And again: "He is remarkably adroit at drawing resentment to himself to divert it from me or one of my clients." Archie uses his note book in this one, but he says that "the only difference between me and a tape recorder is that a tape recorder can't lie. I lie to Wolfe only on matters that are none of his business." "I never do remember anything in the morning until I have washed and showered and shaved and dressed and made my way down to the kitchen. With the orange juice the fog begins to lift, and with the coffee it's all clear. It's a good thing Wolfe breakfasts in his room, on a tray taken up by Fritz, and then goes up to the plant rooms. If we met before breakfast he would have fired me or I would have quit long ago." About the orange juice, by the way, Archie takes it "at room temperature". "Not long ago I got a letter from a woman who had read some of my accounts of Nero Wolfe's activities, asking me why I was down on marriage. . . . I wrote her that as far as I knew there was absolutely nothing wrong with marriage; the trouble was the way people handled it." Archie always cleans up his desk each night: "I refuse to meet a cluttered desk in the morning." Finally, "I will go beyond the call of duty in a pinch, but I wouldn't drink gin and ginger ale to get the lowdown on Lizzie Borden."

OTHER REGULARS ::: "I had summoned Saul Panzer, Fred Durkin, Orrie Cather, and Johnny Keems. . . . They were out four main standbys, and they would call for a daily outlay of $160." Since Archie says elsewhere that Saul "is the best operative alive and rates sixty bucks a day", Fred, Orrie and Johnny must be in the $30-40 per day range.

I was pleased to see that Saul Panzer was in the red leather chair. Unquestionably Johnny Keems had made a go for it, and Wolfe himself must have shooed him off. Johnny, who at one time, under delusions of grandeur, had decided my job would look better on him or he would look better on it, no matter which, but had found it necessary to abandon the idea, was a pretty good operative but had to be handled. Fred Durkin, big and burly and bald, knows exactly what he can expect of his brains and what he can't, which is more than you can say for a lot of people with a bigger supply. Orrie Cather is smart, both in action and in appearance. As for Saul Panzer, I thoroughly approve of his preference for free-lancing, since if he decided he wanted my job he would get it--or anybody else's

. . .

There are things about Saul I don't understand and never will. For instance, the old cap he always wears. If I wore that cap while tailing a subject I'd be spotted in the first block. If I wore it while calling on people for information they would suspect I was cuckoo or quaint and draw the curtains. But Saul never gets spotted unless he wants to, and for extracting material from people's insides nothing can equal him except a stomach pump.

In this episode Saul bows to a woman: "That's another thing about him, his bow; it's as bad as his cap." "Saul's face will never tell you a damn thing when he's playing poker with you, or playing anything that calls for cover, but he's not so careful with it when he doesn't have to be." At one point Saul reports that he "identified" himself to a witness, bringing forth this observation from Archie: "You should hear Saul identifying himself. What he meant was that after three minutes with the doorman they were on such good terms that he was allowed to take the elevator without a phone call to announce him. It's no good trying to imitate him; I've tried it." Saul uses the ejaculation, "jumping Jesus". Note, above, that Fred has been replaced by Saul as the rightful user of the red chair. One other item on Fred Durkin: "Fred never takes his eyes off of Wolfe. I think he's expecting him to sprout either a horn or a halo, I'm not sure which, and he doesn't want to miss it." And, of course, Johnny Keems. Johnny was never a very likeable fellow, and his last days were no different from those which preceeded them. First off, Johnny "titters", but we'll let that pass. "Wolfe was brusque. You have to be brusque with Johnny." Wolfe tells Johnny to "confer with me at once" if he turns up anything. "I have known you to overstrain your talents." And when Johnny fails to report in, Wolfe says "confound him, he's too set on a master stroke." What he is, by this time, is dead, and, to be frank, no one much mourns his passing. Wolfe says that Archie and Saul "were friends and colleagues of Johnny Keems--and I myself knew Keems some years and had esteem for him", but real grief is noticeably absent. We get a few glimpses at Fritz, but only two items merit mention: "Wolfe tells me there was a man in Marseilles who made a better omelet than Fritz, but I don't believe it." And second, Archie mentions having "chicken fricasse with dumplings, methodist style", and goes on to say that "Fritz is not a methodist, but his dumplings are plenty good enough for angels." Theodore is mentioned and is actually present in one scene but, as usual, he does not speak. Doc Vollmer is mentioned, but only as the man whose secretary is Helen Grant, with whom Archie speaks briefly on the phone. Archie also speaks to Lon Cohen on the phone. Nathaniel Parker puts in an appearance. Wolfe says "I have delt with him many years, and I recommend him without reservation." Archie gives Parker's phone number as PHoenix 5-2382 this time. Del Bascom's name is just mentioned, as is that of the Harland Ide Detective Agency. And Lily makes another appearance: "I was only half an hour late joining the gathering at Lily Rowan's table at the Flamingo Club. We followed the usual routine, deciding after a couple of hours that the dance floor was too crowded and moving to Lily's penthouse, where we could do our own crowding." Archie gets home "around three o'clock." Of the official regulars, Commissioner Skinner shows up, as does "Assistant District Attorney Mandelbaum, who had once been given a bigger dose by Wolfe than he could swallow." Cramer, of course, drops around: "'Hello, Goodwin. Wolfe in?' That was a form of wit. He knew damn well Wolfe was in, since he never went out." "He and Wolfe were glaring at each other. They do that from force of habit. Which way they go from the glare, toward a friendly exchange of information or toward a savage exchange of insults, depends on the circumstances." Archie mentions "Cramer's sharp gray eyes, surrounded by crinkles." Regarding Cramer's cigars: "I have never seen him light one"; and, "Cramer threw the chewed cigar at my waste basket, missing as usual." "Wolfe invited him to have some beer and he accepted, I knew he didn't have to be asked how they were making out. They weren't. He takes Wolfe's beer only when he wants it un-erstood that he's only human and should be treated accordingly." After Wolfe solves this one Cramer mellows so much as to call Archie by his first name. Purley is present, too, displaying more hostility than usual toward Wolfe: "Purley rumbled. He was always hoarser than normal in Wolfe's presence, from the strain of controlling his impulses. Or rather, one impulse, the one to find out how many clips it would take to make Wolfe incapable of speech."

PHYSICAL ASPECTS ::: The most startling physical aspect of this case is the fact that the second and third floors have changed places. Wolfe tells a woman "how pleasant our south room was, directly under his with a good bed and morning sunshine." This is not an isolated slip. Archie says he "mounted one flight [from the ground floor] to the South Room. It was too late for sunshine, but it's a nice room even without it." Elsewhere Archie says he "mounted the two flights to my room," which is where it should be, on the third floor. Mention is made of "the table near a window" in Wolfe's bedroom, of billiards in the basement, and of the seven steps of the front stoop. And here's what we have on the roof--"Wolfe wasn't in the first room, the cool one, nor in the second, the medium, nor in the third, the tropical, so I went on through to the potting room." There are some interesting new items regarding the office. "One of my sixteen thousand duties is keeping a five-week file of the *Times* in a cupboard below the bookshelves." The cupboard, incidentally, has sliding doors. There is another cupboard there, too: "Saul and Fred had assembled a kit of tools from the cupboard in the office where we kept an assortment of everything from keys to jimmies." There is a clock on the wall of the office, and on the office floor . . . "He [Wolfe] cocked his head to survey the Feraghan, which covered the central expanse, 14x26." Archie mentions "the door of the bathroom in the corner" of the office, and he says "Wolfe was standing over by the bookshelves, looking at the glove, which was even bigger around than he was." The door to the office is soundproofed, but the dining room door is not, which contradicts Archie's statement in an earlier episode that all of the ground floor of the brownstone is soundproofed.

ROUTINE AT THE BROWNSTONE ::: "With the chain bolt on as usual during my absence, Fritz had to come to let me in"; this happens twice in this episode, in the daytime. It appears to be definitely Archie's duty to answer the doorbell in this one. "I went to the office and switched a light on for a glance at my desk, where Wolfe leaves a note if there is something that needs early-morning attention." Wolfe "rang for beer, two short and one long." Archie tells us "I joined Wolfe in the dining room at seven-fifteen as usual", which establishes the starting time for evening meals, and the following establishes the duration: "Par for Wolfe from clams to cheeze is an hour and a half." Archie also mentions "lunch at one-thirty on Friday", which seems to suggest that it is at times other than one-thirty on other days. Here's a long one:

> How much Wolfe likes to show the orchids to people depends on who it is. Gushers he can stand, and even jostlers. The only ones he can't bear are those who pretend they can tell a P. stuartiana from a P. schilleriana but can't. And there is an ironclad rule that except for Fritz and me, and of course Theodore, who is there all the time, no one goes to the plant rooms for any other purpose than to look at orchids.
>
> Since he refuses to interrupt his two daily turns up there for a trip down to the office, no matter who or what, there have been some predicaments over the years. Once I chased a woman who was part gazelle clear to the top of the second flight before I caught her. The rule hasn't been broken more than half a dozen times altogether, and that afternoon was one of them. [The cause being Herold's attempt to worm out of paying Wolfe for finding his son.] . . . I used the elevator instead of the stairs because the noise it made would notify Wolfe that something drastic was happening.

ODDS & ENDS ::: Wolfe *et cie*. have "chicken livers and mushrooms in white wine. Rice cakes" for lunch one day. A woman stays in the South Room until the killer is caught. Wolfe is in the 80% tax bracket. His fee on this one is $16,666.66, though the client has to pay out an even $50,000 altogether. Lastly: "Selma Hays moved to the corner of Wolfe's desk and said she had to kiss him. She said she doubted if he wanted to be kissed, but she simply had to. Wolfe shook his head. 'Let us forego it. Kiss Mr. Goodwin instead; it will be more to the point.'"

IT'S ABOUT CRIME

NOTES ON RECENT READING

By Marvin Lachman

Dover has outdone itself by reprinting (it is the first U.S. publication) H. Douglas Thomson's *Masters of Mystery: A Study of the Detective Story* (1931). This was the first attempt to publish a book-length history and critique of the detective story, and it is still readable almost fifty years later. Thomson was knowledgeable and wrote with a delightfully subtle sense of humor. He is especially good regarding bad writing, cliches, and some of the absurdities of the thriller. His book abounds in astute observations--e.g., "The detective story is not popular because it is badly written, but badly written because it is popular." His ability to turn a phrase is outstanding--"If detection in real life were stranger and more exciting than detection in fiction, fiction would give up the struggle. It would be the survival of the more fitting."

At times his observations make one wish Thomson had brought his work up to date; he did not die until 1975. He observed that World War I was the nadir of the detective story because of the public's reaction to the wholesale carnage then taking place in real life. I wonder how he would have accounted for the great popularity of mysteries among the British, especially during the "Blitz" in World War II.

There is one major weakness in Thomson's book. He gives away the plots and the murderers of many of the books he discusses. *Trent's Last Case*, *The Cask*, *The French Powder Mystery*, and many other books may be spoiled for unsuspecting readers. It is possible (I've been doing it for more than a decade) to discuss books and authors without giving too much away. It does require a little extra work. Unfortunately, Thomson was either not willing to expend the effort or was insensitive to the fact that detective fiction depends on surprise and the reader not knowing the culprit. Remove those elements and you remove much of the mystery's reason for being. It was unreasonable if he assumed readers would have read all of the books he discussed.

E. F. Bleiler, responsible for this book and so many previous Dover reprints, must be faulted for permitting this to happen without at least warning readers in his introduction. While Bleiler includes footnotes correcting errors, chiefly of fact, committed by Thomson, he did not catch all possible errors. Christie's *The Mysterious Mr. Quin* is not a novel. John Buchan's book had more than *Twenty-Nine* (sic) *Steps*. *The Casebook of Sherlock Holmes* was published ten years later than 1917.

In his introduction, Mr. Bleiler minimizes the importance of "fairness" in writing the detective story, something to which Thomson gave considerable attention. Fairness, of course, refers to the author providing the reader with all information necessary to arrive at a solution to the crime at the same time as the detective. Bleiler fails to get at the reason "fair play" probably no longer exists. It is much more difficult for a writer to plot (and write) a mystery fair to the reader. Ah, but how much more satisfying it is to be able to play that grand game in competition with Ellery

Queen or Hercule Poirot.

Even if you choose, as I did, to skip over discussions of books I haven't read yet (the titles are all italicized), there is much to read and enjoy here. Mystery fans owe an enormous debt to Mr. Bleiler for rescuing a book so important to the genre we love so dearly.

Edgar Wallace was incredibly popular at the time Thomson wrote though he never was as successful in the U.S. as he was (and still is) in England and Germany. Most critics, including Thomson, remark on Wallace's prolificacy. Yet, despite this great output, Wallace often wrote with skill and imagination. His *Double Dan* (1924) is one of the funniest mysteries I've read. Although ultimately the plot is too sparse and the "gimmick" dragged out too long, there is real humor on almost every page. I especially enjoyed Julius Superbus, private investigator and the last Roman in Britain. Wallace's *Day of Uniting* (1926) adeptly combines mystery and science fiction in a plot to end the world.

Jack Finney has written some imaginative mysteries and science fiction--e.g., *Assault on a Queen* and *Invasion of the Body Snatchers*. His *Time and Again* (1970) combines both genres in a novel about a 1970 government project to send a man back to 1882. Finney writes like a dream. As a bonus, his book is illustrated with some vintage photographs from New York history.

Dick Francis is the mystery writer I am most willing to recommend to non-mystery readers. He is one of the great story tellers of all time. *Smokescreen* is one of his best recent books. It has a hero who *is* a hero and many insights into life in South Africa.

W. Somerset Maugham's *Ashenden* (1928) is famous as a volume of connected espionage short stories. I recently read the 1951 Avon edition which was advertised inaccurately as a novel. It is an overrated book due to an almost complete absence of action, minimal plotting, and unsuccessful attempts at surprising, ironic endings. Yet it is interesting to see Maugham presage John Le Carre by presenting a non-glamorous picture of spying. The best part of the book is its insight into Maugham in the thinly disguised person of the hero, Ashenden. We learn much of his attitude toward women, his philosophy, and his reading tastes. What booklover can't identify with the following description: "He passed a good deal of time in the bookshops turning over the pages of books that would have been worth reading if life were a thousand years long."

Avon's slightly misleading advertising was a very mild annoyance compared to my experience with P.D. James' *Cover Her Face*, as published in paperback by Popular Library. Arriving at page 96, I found the next page to be 129. Somehow, an entire signature (32 pages) was omitted. I got my money back from Classic Book Store but am still looking for a complete copy.

While on the subject of publishers' failings, I should mention the typos on almost every page of Robert B. Parker's Edgar-winning *Promised Land* as reprinted by Berkeley. Parker is one of the best writers of Private Eye novels around. His *Mortal Stakes* (1975), which I recently read, is just as good, and was very timely at the time, with its baseball background. However, there are three weaknesses in Parker's Spenser series:

1. Spenser is too much the gourmet, and his preoccupa-

tions with food do not add enough realism to compensate for their intrusions on plot.
  2. Spenser consistently "double crosses" his clients. He accepts an assignment and then either withholds information or goes contrary to the instructions he has received, albeit for what he considers moral reasons.
  3. Too often problems are resolved by violence--not detection. Here, too, it is easier to write action scenes than closely reasoned deduction. It is not always more satisfying to read.
  Peter Styles in Hugh Pentecost's *A Murder Arranged* (1978) also displayes an employer-be-damned attitude. Sent as investigative reporter (what an "in" expression that has become) to a small Connecticut town where a murder took place, he quickly decides to help prove the innocence of the accused without really doing much objective investigation. Again, there is very little detection, only an "action" scene as denouement.
  Lest we think only America has this kind of book, take Gil North's *Sergeant Cluff Stands Firm* (1960), only published in England. Caleb Cluff is enraged at the murder of a "nice" person, but his investigation barely gets off the ground. Still, with few clues, the murderer is discovered, and there is a violent ending. Incidentally, the unusual publisher of this paperback is TRUST, a subsidiary of OXFAM, the Oxford Famine Relief Fund.
  In *The Noose* (1930) by Philip MacDonald, Colonel Gethryn becomes convinced of a young man's innocence five days before he is scheduled to be hung. There is a tremendous sense of immediacy to this book because of the deadline imposed, and that is rare in mysteries. Unfortunately, Gethryn solves the case with minimal detection though he is very busy. There is more detection in *The Link* (1930), but the book is slow, and the narrator, Michael Lawless, weakens Gethryn's role. What passes as American slang is ludicrous without being funny. There were many errors in the almost 50 year old British Crime Club edition I read.
  The Gothic is still with us. The heroine in Barbara Michaels' *Wait for What Will Come* (1978) inherits a castle in Cornwall. She wanders around, alone, and someone scares the hell out of her by hanging seaweed in her room. In a concession to the 70's, Ms. Michaels makes here somewhat aware of sex and even has her say "I do consider drugs somewhat perverse, anything beyond an occasional joint."
  Overlooked is the Gothic hero--e.g. Willie Foley in Michael Kenyon's *May You Die in Ireland* (1965). He is a 40 year old math professor who is baldish and overweight and is given to chivalrous, erotic fantasies. A promisingly realistic hero. Then he inherits an Irish castle and begins to act dumb, trusting everyone and wandering alone into danger.
  Brian Garvield, with the assistance of Dorothy Salisbury Davis and MWA, has come up with a unique idea for a true crime anthology in *I, Witness* (N.Y. Times Books, 1978). Twenty-five writers tell of their own encounters with real crime. Sometimes, as in Aaron Marc Stein's "involvement" in the Wylie-Hoffert killings or Robert Bloch on the case that inspired *Psycho*, the Writer had little to do with the events. On the other hand, John Ball as victim of an armed robbery could easily have lost his life. Other crimes are more trivial but nonetheless worth telling (and reading) about--e.g. Lawrence Treat as victim of dirty politics on Martha's Vin-
(Continued on p. 16)

MYSTERY*FILE

Short Reviews by Steve Lewis

Charles Merrill Smith, *Reverend Randollph and the Avenging Angel* (Putnam's, 1977; 245 pp.).

    Rev Randollph, once a quarterback for the L.A. Rams, is now interim pastor for Chicago's famous Church of the Good Shepherd, learning first hand how real life differs from that of the seminary. Included as a part of his education is this, his second case of murder, of a new bride once an extremely close friend.

    Besides understanding people and revealing what good deal he knows of human relationships, Smith certainly dispels a lot of the unwarranted veneration laymen have toward the clergy. The murder investigation gets short shrift, but the subtle rewards shown accruing to religious life can only be described as spiritually uplifting. (A minus)* [This and all subsequent reviews marked with an asterisk have appeared earlier in the *Hartford Courant*.]

Celia Fremlin, *The Spider-Orchid* (Crime Club, 1977; U.S. 1978; 185 pp.).

    The accustomed solitary routine of a recently divorced man is suddenly disrupted when his mistress proudly announces that her husband has finally agreed to let her go, but when she moves in, the results are even worse than he expected. Fremlin does well in building up characters while tearing down the relationships between them, and she manages to keep the reader in a considerable amount of suspense even though it's a long time before murder (or any other real crime) is committed. Several of the ominous hints of incipient violence along the way turn out instead to have been misleading, however, and so they were a mistake, for the seeds of disaster were more firmly planted than I think even Fremlin realized. (B minus)

Hartshorne, *The Mexican Assassin* (Scribner's, 1977, 1978; a different version was published in England by Robert Hale, Ltd., 1977; 247 pp.).

    I've never wanted to go to Mexico, not that I ever had the chance to, but this non-advertisement for the miserably hot climate of our neighbor south of the border and the reflected glare of the rampant poverty in a land governed by greed and corruption hasn't a chance in hell of convincing me otherwise. There are those there who still harbor hopes of revolution, and to tell the truth, my sympathies are with them, supposing that it could be done without outside assistance, and that it would do any good. I suspect that the pseudonymous Hartshorne, described on the dust jacket as once having held a sensitive position in U.S. intelligence, feels much the same way.

    But what a pleasure it is to read some "spy fiction" that's well-written--and how tempting it is to add "for a change"--especially when it comes from the typewriter of someone obviously an insider to the dirty tricks and the grubby political maneuvering that can only occur with the full knowledge and encouragement of those in key positions. Someone might inform Hartshorne, however, even though he's probably very much aware of it, that long one-sided monologues back and forth do not a conversation make.

As for the story, the adventures of an undercover agent working without the full support of his unnamed agency while burrowed into a village and a country more than a little suspicious of all foreigners always lead to top-notch suspense, even though there's not a great deal to be added that's never been said before, but again, neither did I start another book while this one was in progress. (A minus)

Reginald Bretnor, *A Killing in Swords* (Pocket 81313, 1978; 214 pp.).

So far as I know, this book was never on sale in the Hartford area. I had to go all the way to Massachusetts for a copy, but even though Bretnor is pretty well-known to longtime readers of science fiction, I'm awfully glad that that's not the only reason I drove so far on such a hot day.

I read a lot of mysteries, as you may have noticed, but there aren't many that are actually hard work to read. This one was, and it's hard even to find anything good to say about it.

Doing the detective work is a San Francisco antique weapons dealer named Alastair Alexandrovitch Timuroff, which right away explains the overpowering Continental accent that only someone with a name like Zsa Zsa can get away with, and wouldn't you know it, every last one of the suspects and all of the other main characters collect either swords, knives, guns or some other sort of lethal object. Dead is the city's mayor, with his pants down, evidently while he was trying to mount one of the ultra-realistic mechanical women populating the home of eccentric genius inventor Dr. Grimwood.

I'm serious. And I think Bretnor was, too. There is a question of locked doors, but maybe not, since that part of the case was never followed up. With all the secret doors and passageways infiltrating the place, it probably doesn't really matter.

What Bretnor seems to have been aiming for is the vintage flavor of 1930s Queen or Philo Vance, but perhaps writing a mystery story is harder than people think. Bizarre events and weird characters are not what I want in a detective story. I want people who can think logically instead of careening around in idle chit-chat. I want an investigation carried on by first-hand observation and personal interrogation and not indirectly through rumors and suppositions and half-baked accusations. I don't want pages and pages on pseudo-Indian religions. Dirty limericks, well, OK, maybe.

Enough. What else can I say? This is a book awful enough to be rotten without yet being awful enough for it to be read and enjoyed for its own sake. Avoid. (F)

Robert Aickman, *Cold Hand in Mine* (Scribner's, 1975; U.S. 1977; 252 pp.).

These eight tales are billed as English ghost stories, which is a little misleading. They are indeed very English, but you'd have to stretch your imagination to its inner depths before finding any trace of a preconceived "ghost". Which is exactly what Aickman has in mind--to illustrate the chilling conjurations a mind can create out of a situation which suddenly veers out of the ordinary into the subtly bizarre. No explanations offered, most wisely, so beware of letting these enigmatic mysteries creep under your skin. Not, I'm sure, to everyone's taste--horror stories written to also be read on a symbolic level will have only limited appeal--but in likewise limited doses they surely and quietly expand the restrictions of the genre. (B)*

Joan Fleming, *Every Inch a Lady* (Putnam's, 1977; 193 pp.).
Easter Cragg, although brought up an orphan, seems hardy the kind of lady to be the center of so much homicidal activity, but after the murders of both her husband and then her doting father-in-law, and in spite of a surprising lack of curiosity or thirst for revenge on her part, a new neighbor and admirer is compelled to continue working on her behalf. Many a false trail lies in waiting, catching the reader's interest in peripheral matters, necessarily so, as the slayings themselves turn out to have disappointingly little mystery to them. (C plus)*

Brian Freeborn, *Ten Days, Mister Cain?* (St. Martin's, 1977; 185 pp.).
Harry Grant, a small-time London con-man who successfully impersonated a notorious hit man named Cain in his previous adventure, finds that selfsame gentleman hot on his trail in this one. That, plus some unlikely spy stuff involving the Foreign Office, gives Harry plenty to sweat about, but while the slangy cockney style reads true, it's awfully tough on Americans, particularly those asking for something a lot more substantial to get involved with. (F)*

James Follett, *Crown Court* (St. Martin's, 1977; U.S. 1978; 174 pp.).
An unemployed used-car dealer, called in for jury duty just as his wife is due to give birth to their first child, is a reluctant witness to several brief cenarios of British justice--a case involving a thriving pornography business, a scuba-diving murder affair, and the unexpected intrusion of international terrorism, all while complications set in at the hospital down the street. Two-dimensional television drama, gripping for the moment, and then instantly forgettable. (C plus)*

Stuart Kaminsky, *Murder on the Yellow Brick Road* (St. Martin's 1977, 197 pp.).
"Someone had murdered a Munchkin." So begins the latest case of Toby Peters, last seen helping Errol Flyn out of a nasty blackmail scheme. This time it's a frightened Judy Garland who demands that MGM allow our lowly Hollywood private eye to handle the affair.
Name-dropping is again as much of a nuisance as it is of nostalgia value, but rather amusing is the assistance of a rather famous mystery writer who happens to be in Hollywood at the time. More importantly, by the time he's cracked the case, this time the raffish Toby Peters has begun to become a little more real himself, in a way equivalent to catching a glimpse of an actual person hidden behind the glitter and glamor visible up front on the silver screen.
Next, the Marx Brothers. (B minus)*

Peter Lovesey, *Waxwork* (Pantheon, 1978; 240 pp.).
Mystery fiction written before the turn of the century is doubtless an acquired taste, one that I've never developed. Yet with smooth and consummate ease Lovesey continues to show that not only can detective stories be successfully set in the days of Queen Victoria, but he also blends the details of

this long-ago era into an essential part of the crime and its solution. In this, his lates, all Britain eagerly awaits the salacious details as a beautiful woman is accused of poisoning a blackmailer and is committed for trial at Old Bailey. Sergeant Cribb's task is to close out the investigation--some details remain that could yet contradict the lady's guilty plea.

From a technical sense, this had to be one of the most difficult tales to tell of any in recent months, and as the jiggery-pokery at length slides effortlessly into place, one can only sit back and applaud with admiration. (A)*

Kin Platt, *The Screwball King Murder* (Random House, 1978; 184 pp.).

Private eye Max Roper's latest sports-related caper involves the not-so-accidental drowning of a flaky left-hander who had just signed a million-dollar contract to pitch for the Los Angeles Dodgers. Murder follows Roper like a well-trained puppy, but baseball fans will be disappointed to learn that the motive for Hondo Kenyon's death really lies in the totally antithetical world of skin flicks and acid rock. Slick, and superficial, detective work. (C)*

Jacqueline Wilson, *Making Hate* (St. Martins, 1977; U.S. 1978; 189 pp.).

Few crimes are more degrading than that of rape, and seldom does the pain and humiliation end when the rapist is finished with the victim's body. Times are changing, however. The crudeness of the investigators' approach now lies more in the implications of questions like, "Did you cooperate with the assailant?"

Both the initial suspect and a key to the capture of the troubled mind responsible for a series of London assaults is Simon Shaw, a civilian police assistant who gathers fingerprints, pieces of glass and so on after a crime. This may indeed be the first time that one of these anonymous men actually has a major role in solving a detective story--can anyone name another? Simon has a home life, too, the highlight being a series of Sunday reunions with his children. In addition to being a remarkably accurate police procedural, the plus here is nicely wrought human drama. (A minus)*

George Bagby, *The Tough Get Going* (Crime Club, 1977; 178 pp.).

A friend of Bagby's, a top-notch investigative reporter, turns up floating in the East River, right after a mysterious, nearly incoherent visit late the night before. He may have been drugged, but before he hust as mysteriously disappeared, he asked Bagby not to notify the FBI or CIA, not even Inspector Schmidt.

Bagby, also known as Aaron Marc Stein, writes better than he plots. I read this stuff non-stop. An hour later, I'm hungry again. (B minus)

Michael Collins, *The Nightrunners* (Dodd, Mead, 1978; 216 pp.).

One-armed private detective Dan Fortune is hired to track down a wandering husband possessed by a compulsive mania for gambling, but bit by bit the full story is revealed--one of drugs, money, Bolivian rebels, and murder. This once enjoyable series is being done in by its own author, however, as Collins concentrates far too long on the tortured agony of the past, and the life in the shadows of what isn't and never was, and neglects his more important job, that of keeping the reader involved. (D)*

Colin Watson, *Charity Ends at Home* (Berkley, 1969; 160 pp.).
   Flaxborough seems to be a quiet sort of town, if such a description can, after all, apply to a place that attracts much more than its share of murders, with only mild cases of eccentricity afflicting the majority of its inhabitants. Nothing gets done right away of its own accourd, for, you see, "Perhaps It'll Go Away" is not a bad motto to live by--thinking in this case primarily of Chief Constable Chubb, who is the first to get one of the unsigned letters sent to various townspeople warning them somehow of the writer's impending doom.
   Inspector Purbright seems a little more alert than some of the other folks around, but it does seem a little more than miraculous that he can make anything at all of this affair, befuddled as it quickly becomes by an incipient war building up between various charity organizations on the streets of Flaxborough and by a persistent and mendacious private detective all the way from London.
   It's a nice little scheme that's been put into action--bewildering in spots while very easily seen through in others. I was fooled nicely, I have to admit, by the above-mentioned letters, but not in the least, I hasten to add, by who done it. (C plus)

Phyllis A. Whitney, *Mystery of the Angry Idol* (Signet, 1965; 176 pp.).
   One of the better of the few tourist attractions that Connecticut has to offer is Mystic Seaport, a restored version of what seaports and ship-building centers of days gone by were like, complete with ships, shops, and exhibits of all sorts. And it's difficult to picture a more beautiful setting for a lonely 12-year-old girl to fina a mystery in, one that Jan Pendleton is plunged into on her very first day of separation from her parents and her younger twon brothers.
   While her father serves an overseas tour of duty, she's to stay with her **grandmother and her 90-year-old great-grandmother--hardly the sort of companions a lively, inquisitive girl would** wish upon herself. But her great-grandmother's collection of jade from China, the mysterious inscription upon a hideous masked idol, and the housekeeper's son with the sharp scent of scandal about him all soon help her forget her loneliness.
   The secret of the idol is an obvious one, and I think most kids reading this book will have it figured out long before the four generations of Pendletons do. I don't imagine that most boys will admit to enjoying this book, even if you can get them to read it, since it's about a girl and especially because it does get a little soppy-eyed toward the end, but I suspect that both boys and girls will feel a close kinship to a peer whose elders just don't understand her and who are most singularly unfair in the decisions they make. Even to my mind the great-grandmother's abrupt change in attitude toward Jan seems to be a case of going too far, necessary only to satisfy some need of the author at that point, and the explanation later is noticeably weak.
   In all other ways, however, I can't think of how something written for younger teen-agers could make a stronger case for books as constant friends. The thrill of reading is

one that can always be returned to, and it's one I think that I've always known. (B)

Michael Innes, *The Case of Sonia Wayward* (Dodd Mead, 1960; 218 pp.).

It begins with Sonia dead, no mourning her. She had been a prolific writer of romances, trifles to be sure, but quite popular with certain segments of the population, and quite naturally Colonel Pettigate, her husband of long standing and forbearance, finds the need to carry on without her.

As he blithely blithers his way through her unexpected absence, leaving gaping holes carelessly strewn as he passes, he does manage to complete Sonia's latest work-in-progress, giving rise as he does so to a good deal of deft tongue-in-check tom-foolery about the mysterious ways of artistic creation. But at length blackmail and the social graces suggest that Sonia's return, for at most a week, say, would do wonders for the colonel's growing embarrassments. Of course there's an obvious way out, one that not even the colonel can miss.

It ends as a high-brow comedy, delicious and wholly captivating, though I shouldn't say that many will be at all surprised with the ensuing vicissitudes of fate. Innes prepares us for them especially well in advance. (A minus)

(Continued from p. 2) started with the middle pages and did the cover last; I think you can see that I did make progress, though not without a relapse here and there. I hope I can remember enough to get out an entirely legible issue this time.

Apologies also to Frank Hamilton for failing to give him credit for last issue's cover. Sorry, Frank, but in the rush of typing the editorial and the contents page I entirely overlooked it.

Time now for some brisk wrist slapping. This issue should have contained two reports on Bouchercon 9. It contains one. Mary Ann Grochowski, who reported on last year's Bouchercon for TMF, was busy with her bookselling activities during most of this year's convention and so was unable to report on the program. She did, however, prepare a report on the unprogramed aspects of the convention which I think you will all enjoy. When I learned that Mary Ann would be unable to do a full report, I asked Don Yates if he would undertake it and he graciously agreed. Unfortunately, that gracious agreement was the last thing I got out of Don except for a short note six weeks ago saying that he would mail the report in the next few days. Even one of my finely crafted limericks-- "There was a professor named Yates," etc.--has failed to produce results, so there is no report on the Bouchercon program in this issue. I did a report myself for Iwan Hedman's *Dast*, and if I don't hear from Don soon I'll ask Iwan if I can reprint that report in TMF--unless someone else has a report they can submit. I took some photographs--not good ones, I fear--which I was going to use to illustrate Don's article. Perhaps I'll be able to work them into the next issue, too.

VERDICTS
(More Reviews)

Jeffrey Archer, *Shall We Tell the President?* (Viking, 1977).
   Marc Andrews, special agent, is the sole surviving member of a triumvirate of FBI agents interviewing an illegal Greek immigrant who has information of a plot to assassinate President M. Kennedy in this novel set in the year 1983. As his partner and superior have been killed in a car crash and the Greek murdered in the hospital, Andrews must race to find which of the 100 Senators in Congress has helped plan the coup. Becoming the personal operative of the FBI Director, Andrews must search through mountains of records to narrow the range of suspects, his problems compounded by his love for the daughter of one of his prime Senate suspects. The result is a taut tale of suspense and detection, culminating in a dramatic confrontation on the steps of the Capital. (Thomas L. Motsinger)

Bill Pronzini and Collin Wilcox, *Twospot* (Putnam's, 1978; 268 pp.).
   This started out as a good idea: take Pronzini's "nameless" (whose name turns out to be, as we suspected, Bill) and Wilcox's Lt. Hastings and turn them loose on the same case. Most of the time, the good idea works. The story is told in alternating sections by "nameless" and Hastings, and the authors' styles blend well; both are first-person narrations, but the styles are distinctive. No one is likely to wonder just who's telling the story at a given time. The thing about the book to which I objected was its assassination theme, about which I will say no more--and don't read the dust jacket. Anyway, I've just about had it with assassinations. The only attempted assassination that hasn't been done in fiction by this time is that of the mayor of Cut-and-Shoot, Texas, and someone may be working on that. It's too bad that two good writers didn't pick a better story to write. (Bill Crider)

Fred Saberhagen, *The Holmes-Dracula File*. (Ace, 1978, 249 pp.).
   What new evil walks the streets of London? What fiend threatens the very existence of the Empire?
   Well, not necessarily Dracula, in spite of what the title leads you to believe. Oh, the Count is present, all right, and even alternates chapters with the good Doctor Watson, and, to be sure, he's about his bloody business. But there is more. For this, my friends, is the true, finally revealed story of The Giant Rat of Sumatra. And what a story! Weird! Weird! Weird! You may also add Fun! Fun! Fun! to that.
   In this clever, and long overdue meeting of minds, Saberhagen gives us yet another adventure of Mr. Holmes and his loyal Watson, and presents us with a quite different sort of Dracula.
   Is this the same "foul" night creature that gave Van Helsing so much hell?
   The story begins with an old man being clubbed on the docks and taken away for experiments. Experiments that involve rats--tons of them! But the old man seems considerably different from what you would expect of most geezers. There is something very peculiar and hypnotic about this bloke.

And just when some of these peculiarities are about to be explained . . . switch to the comfortable, tobacco reeked apartments of Holmes and Watson, and to a rather oddball letter that Holmes holds in his hands. A letter dealing with a missing person and a giant rat!

And so Holmes enters upon this until now unchronicled case; and in that strange way of literary mysteries, it crosses with the problems of the old man. I won't be giving away any secrets by revealing this old man as Count Dracula, since that is rather obvious from the start, but suffice it to say there becomes a common interest between the two. Dracula is out to correct a rather crude mishandling of his person (are vampires persons?), and in so doing entangles in the Master Sleuth's sleuthing.

Tremendous fun and highly recommended. (A-) (Joe Lansdale)

John Buchan, *The Thirty-nine Steps* (Introduction by Michael F. Gilbert; bibliography by Janet Adam Smith; illustrations by Karl Nicholason; Del Mar: University Extension, University of California, San Diego/Publisher's Inc, 1978; 158 pp.;$6.95)

The Mystery Library continues to pick well-known books for their series with this, their eighth book. I suspect that one of the reasons this book was chosen was because of economy; it is an *extremely* short book, and the publishers needed to increase the type size in order to fill a hundred and fifty-eight pages of text. Even though the book is short, it's still welcome; it's nice to see an old friend back in print.

The Thirty-nine Steps anticipates many of the chase-spy adventure thrillers of the last fifty years. It could be argued that nearly every book of this sort (and certainly most of the spy novels) either derives much of their techniques from Buchan (Geoffrey Household being the most prominent acolyte) or is a conscious reaction to Buchan's romanticism (Eric Ambler having admitted as much, he being in many ways Household's antithesis). Here we find the familiar themes of the lonely man, beset on all sides, battling against his enemies. Buchan had more than a trace of the conspiratorial and paranoia in his works, admittedly; but his heroes always triumph, and do not sink in fear and terror. *The Thirty-nine Steps* is a *good* book--moral without being preachy, exciting without excessive violence. I urge all of you to read it and its three sequels, *Greenmantle, Mr. Steadfast* and *The Three Hostages*.

As for the appendices, Michael Gilbert contributes a fine introduction, keenly analysing Buchan's methods and manners with an incisive wit. Gilbert has written very little criticism (at least for American audiences) but when he does write is always worthwhile, and he should be encouraged to do more. The "List of Books by John Buchan" is apparently a reprint of the list from Janet Adam Smith's biography of Buchan, although there is no notice of this on the copyright page. There is also a reprint from TAD by J. Randolph Cox, and the usual reprints of reviews of the time. We then spend nearly half the critical space allotted for this book on stills and criticism of films made from this book, which leads one to wonder if the co-authors of *The Thirty-nine Steps* were Buchan and Alfred Hitchcock. It is stated that "few Americans appear to know *The Thirty-nine Steps* as a novel"; surely the Mystery Library editors know the long and successful record of this book in the marketplace, while most of the books turned by Alfred

Hitchcock into movies have remained in a dusty oblivion. Why put *The Thirty-nine Steps* in the same category as the relatively obscure *Marnie* or *The Rainbird Pattern*? (Story A, Appendices B-) (Martin Morse Wooster)

Christianna Brand, *Green for Danger* (Introduction and annotated bibliography by Otto Penzler; illustrations by Karl Nicholason; Del Mar: University Extension, University of California, San Diego/Publisher's Inc., 1978; 254 pp., $6.95)

The ninth Mystery Library book continues the admirable policy of the Mystery Library of honoring living authors with inclusion in the serious. Previous *Festschriften* have saluted Ellery Queen and Eric Ambler; now we have a somewhat more obscure author getting her share of the glory. Brand was a popular mystery writer in the Forties and Fifties who abandoned detection for personal reasons unknown to me. Since 1955 she has produced Gothics, historicals, short story collections, and three novels featuring Nurse Matilda (*Nurse Matilda, Nurse Matilda Goes to Town* and *Nurse Matilda Goes to Hospital*). Her last novel to be published in this country was *The Radiant Dove*, published by St. Martin's in 1976 as by "Annabel Jones".

Green for Danger is the second in the series of five books detailing the cases of Inspector Cockrill--"Cockie" for short. This novel takes place in a military hospital during the Battle of Britain. After many introductory pages of description and desultory romance, a murder takes place in the operating-room. No one knows why the victim was murdered--he was just a postman with no known connections with any of the six suspects who were in the operating room at the time of his death. Thus, after more fits and starts, Inspector Cockrill is called in. He isolates the suspects, hoping that one of them will crack, and the knots of suspicion gradually grow tighter. After one more murder, an attempted poisoning by gas and an operation supervised (and bungled) by Cockrill, the murderer is disclosed in a particularly nasty denouement.

What we have here is a very late example of classical detection. There is very little violence in the book, and even the operations are daintily handled. When written well, this type of book can be as much a masterpiece as books written in other sub-genres. Brand, though, does not write well; half her suspects are cut out of the came cloth, and her complex web of motives quickly unravels when one is unable to discern any difference between characters. Cockrill does very little detection, and much of what he does is botched. The book, as a whole, is much more narrow-minded than Penzler would have it be; the "time of omnipresent terror and mass death" comes across as little more than the tull thudding of bombs in the distance. Thus we have one of the last of the old style of detective story that takes place in a blissful never-never land, in an old country house or other safe haven far removed from the terrors of the world. That Brand chose to add a touch of realism to the formula shows at once the decadence of the form and the path towards the future.

The appendices are fairly good, though rather thin this time out. Penzler, while a fine editor (even his failures are worth a look), is not, to my taste, a very good critic. Here he continues his bad habits of overusing superlatives and being pompous. (Can anyone who can write a sentence such as "Book critics for many of the English-speaking world's greatest journals found *Green for Danger* worthy of review" *not* be pompous?) Penzler has, though, turned out a fine bibliography--the best, save for Allan Hubin's, in this series--which partially redeems the lack of style and substance in his criticism. Karl Nicholason's illustrations are both badly done and badly produced; he's burning himself out, and one hopes that The Mystery Library hires a new staff artist for future books. (Story C, Appendices B)   (Martin Morse Wooster)

Edward D. Hoch, *The Thefts of Nick Velvet* (Mysterious Press, 1978; 214 pp.; $10 or $20 limited).
    Edward D. Hoch is a phenomemon. He makes his living almost exclusively from short stories, in an age when the short story is supposed to be dying. He's sold over four hundred stories, and has written nearly ten percent of the stories that have appeared in EQMM in this decade. Yet, despite his prodigious production, there have only been three Hoch collections--two obscure paperbacks and *The Spy and the Thief*, published by Davis in 1971. Thus this collection of thirteen short stories is both welcome and important, as the first hardcover collection of Hoch's work.
    Nick Velvet is a professional thief who only steals what he considers to be without value. His standard fee is $20,000-$30,000 for assignments considered particularly dangerous. He also, on occasion, acts as a detective, particularly when foulups occur. There have been, as of the publication date, thirty-four Nick Velvet stories; seven were collected as the "Thief" portion of *The Spy and the Thief*. (Two stories appear in both collections, which is regrettable when one considers the number of unreprinted Velvet stories.)
    "The Theft of the Clouded Tiger" (EQMM, 9/66): Nick Velvet steals a rare white tiger from the zoo, supposedly for a rich oil sheik.
    "The Theft from the Onyx Pool" (EQMM, 6/67): All the water from playwright Samuel Fitzpatrick's swimming pool--in order to discover what secrets lay inside . . . .
    "The Theft of the Toy Mouse" (EQMM, 6/68): Why would the disappearance of a ninety-eight cent toy mouse seriously disrupt a major Hollywood production?
    "The Theft of the Meager Beavers" (EQMM, 12/69): A Caribbean dictator asks Nick Velvet to steal a major league baseball team so that the local team will have someone to play against. Even Nick Velvet thought this plan was odd--and does his best to prevent an interantional incident.
    "The Theft of the Silver Lake Serpent" (Argosy, 1/70): In which a Loch Ness-like monster is stolen from a small New England lake.
    "The Theft of the Seven Ravens" (EQMM, 1/72): The seven ravens in question are the sacred symbol of the Republic of Gola--and Nick Velvet is paid both to guard and steal them. A confusing mixture of theivery and international intrigue.
    "The Theft of the Mafia Cat" (EQMM, 5/72): Mike Pirrone was a leading member of the Syndicate--and Mike Pirrone's cat was his favorite pet. By stealing Mike Pirrone's cat, Velvet takes on the mob, and the story becomes a peculiar sort of inverted detective story.
    "The Theft from the Empty Room" (EQMM, 9/72): Nick Velvet is hired to steal the contents of a storeroom--only the storeroom is empty . . . .
    "The Theft of the Crystal Crown" (*Mike Shayne's*, 1/73): The peaceful Mediterranean island of New Ionia became a revolutionary hotbed when Nick Velvet stole the symbol of sov-

ereignty over the island.
"The Theft of the Circus Poster" (EQMM, 5/73): It was an ordinary circus poster, but could prove if the heir to an oil fortune was what he claimed to be. Here is the search-into-the-past story, in which Velvet becomes detective to dig up some interesting circus history.
"The Theft of Nick Velvet" (EQMM, 2/74): Nick Velvet is kidnapped in order to prevent his services from being used by wealthy industrialist Max Solar. Nick buys his freedom by offering to do another theft--and finds out who "Mas Solar" really is . . . .
"The Theft of the General's Trash" (EQMM, 5/74): Nick Velvet meets Watergate as a muckraking political columnist hires Velvet to steal the trash of a general who doubles as an important White House aide. The story was ruined for me by one scene where Velvet disguises himself as a milkman in order to get into the general's apartment building, when there have been no milk deliveries in Washington for the last ten years.
"The Theft of the Bermuda Penny" (EQMM, 6/75): Nick goes to Saratoga Springs in order to steal a lucky Bermuda penny from compulsive gambler Alfred Cazar. A good rousing fight finishes the tale.
As one can see from the descriptions, Hoch manages to put plenty of variety into his formula. In these stories, we have Velvet acting as a spy, a caper artist, a con man, and as a detective. He visits foreign countries, meets odd people, and does his job well. For Hoch never lets his readers down, always supplying enough intrigue and interest to keep his readers turning the pages. That's why he has sold as many stories as he has, and why we hope he sells many more. A good collection from one of the best short story writers in the mystery field. (B+) (Martin Morse Wooster)

Carroll John Daly, *Murder from the East* (IPL 1002, 1978; 312 pp.; introduction by Tony Sparafucile; originally published by Frederick A. Stokes Co., 1935).
Thanks to International Polygonics Ltd. Library of Crime Classics, Carroll John Daly, the father of fast-action, hard-boiled detective stories, is back in print.
In *Murder from the East* Race Williams, private detective, is hired by a nationally known figure known as "The General" to help stop an oriental takeover of the U.S. Work with--or is it against--Williams is Florence Drummond, known as The Flame, who's married to the leader of the takeover plot.
In his introduction, Tony Sparafucile compares *Murder from the East*, Daly's attempt at a Yellow Peril novel, with Mickey Spillane's crusade against Communism in *One Lonely Night*. Sparafucile also laments Daly's recent neglect in print and compares Spillane's narrative drive as derived from Daly. In this reader's opinion, Sparafucile's comparisons are all just.
Uniform with *Murder from the East* is Baroness Orczy's *The Man in the Corner*. Each book costs $4.00 plus 75¢ each for postage and handling. For those interested in ordering, IPL's address is: IPL, c/o Guinn Company, 70 Hudson St., Hoboken, NJ 07030. (Theodore P. Dukeshire)

James Hadley Chase, *Consider Yourself Dead* (Robert Hale, Ltd., 1978; 188 pp.).
Using his oft-repeated themes of the perfect job gone

wrong and the sometimes vicious family ties of the very rich, James Hadley Chase tells the story of the kidnapping of a billionaire industrialist's daughter.

After an aborted kidnap attempt in Rome, Carlos Grandi sends his daughter, Gina, to an island estate off the Florida coast.

To this island fortress comes Mike Frost, ex-cop with his eye always on getting The Big Money. Getting a job as a security guard presents no problem, but Frost is soon suckered into acting as the inside man by Lu Silk, Mitch Goble, and Ross Umney, three men who intend to kidnap Gina and force her father to hand over to them an illicit Swiss account. Unfortunately for the group, Gina wants Mike to kill her father so she can go and "do her thing". The kidnap scheme comes further unhitched when Gina allows herself to be kidnapped then escapes from the trio of would-be thieves . . . .

Consider Yourself Dead is vintage Chase, this reader couldn't put it down. (Theodore P. Dukeshire)

John Gardner, *To Run a Little Faster* (Sphere Books, 1978; 191 pp.; originally published by Michael Joseph Ltd., 1976).

The recent crop of spy thrillers using World War II is now joined by John Gardner.

Using Anthony Eden's resignation and the British public's refusal to believe there would be another war is the background to this spy thriller.

Michael Hensman, a minor M.P., suddenly disappears, and Simon Darrell is assigned to the story. Following Hensman's trail from London to Basle and back, Darrell and his girlfriend, Poppy, are threatened by both the police and his newspaper to drop the story; but Darrell continues to dig until he finds a connection between Hensman's disappearance and Eden's resignation. Then a third group enters the picture. (Theodore P. Dukeshire)

Jim Thomas, *Cross Purposes* (McCall Publishing, 1971; 188 pp.).

New York based private detective Peter Cross is hired to locate a missing Chinese peach-bloom vase which was stolen.

Cross's search leads him to two beautiful women, one of whom is looking for her missing boyfriend. Warned off the case by two hoods, Cross continues his search and finds a duplicate fase, a small town where he gets beaten, a double-cross, and finally murder before he's able to get the vase back. All in all a good P.I. story; *Cross Purposes* is supposed to be the first of a series which this reader hopes continues. (Theodore P. Dukeshire)

Janwillem Van de Wetering, *The Japanese Corpse* (Houghton, Mifflin Co., 1977; $7.95).

Detective De Gier and the Commissaris travel to Japan to investigate an art fraud leaving Detective Grijpstra in Amsterdam to solve the case of a missing Japanese, whose car is found with blood on the front seat and a dent in the roof from a bullet.

Unless someone is interested in learning about Japan and the life of the people there, it would be best to forget this book. The story drags interminably and the by-play between the two detectives, which, at least, made the earlier Van de Wetering books somewhat humorous, is missing. (Myrtis Broset)

E. X. Ferrars, *The Pretty Pink Shroud* (Doubleday, 1977; $6.95).

A bloodied gown with a bullet hole shows up at a charity shop; the owner of the dress is missing and the villagers suspect the woman was murdered by her husband or has run away with her husband's brother-in-law, who is also missing. The local detective and his fiancee are unwillingly drawn into the case; they question the husband, who seems quite nonchalant about his wife's absence, disclaiming any knowledge as to the reason for the bullet hole in her dress and shows no interest whatsoever in the missing man. The detective will arrive at the answer, but, unfortunately, the reader will already be there.

This is a mild, undramatic story with nothing in it to be enthusiastic about. (Myrtis Broset)

Evelyn Anthony, *The Silver Falcon* (NAL, 1978; $2.25).

Charles Schriber's will, leaving all his possessions, including his beloved horse, the Silver Falcon, to his young wife Elizabeth, has consequences he could not foresee. Elizabeth's life is in danger and a dishonest competitor conspires to prevent The Falcon from winning the Derby at Upsom Downs. Warned against Schriber's son Richard by her husband's good friend and physician, Elizabeth nevertheless falls in love with Richard, finding it impossible to believe that Richard is the maniac he is pictured to be.

Anthony has combined a dramatic story of racing with murder and romance to make this a book for everyone. A suspenseful book that mystery readers won't be able to put down until the finish. (Myrtis Broset)

David Anthony, *Stud Game* (Pocket Books, 1978; $1.75).

David Anthony, who seems to get better with each book, has written here a story of blackmail and murder wherein he introduces a new detective, Stan Bass, tough, yet well-mannered, who, undoubtedly, will be compared to Lew Archer.

A man's car plunges over a cliff, killing him. His widow is later contacted by a pregnant, blonde actress threatening a paternity suit against the dead man unless she receives $100,000. Bass is hired by the man's father to check into the blonde's story. Going to make the pay-off, he finds the actress dead in a swimming poot. The body disappears and the police refuse to believe there was a murder. Bass now insists the earlier death was no accident and turns his investigation toward the dead man's friends. The story comes to a climax when Bass and the killer meet and each tries to outwit the other.

For everyone who enjoys a good mystery or just likes to read about a resourceful detective. (Myrtis Broset)

William Harrison, *Hell's Full* (Manor Books, 1977; $1.75).

The body of old Jesse Stover is found hanging in his barn. Mortician Harry Hooper tries to convince the coroner Stover was murdered but is unsuccessful. The people in the village believe the old man killed his partner and buried the body, now he has committed suicide.

Hooper persists in looking for proof of the murder, though he is shot at, pleaded with by Stover's daughter-in-law to drop the matter and warned by the village mad woman. The only help he receives is from his assistant at the mortuary, who thinks Hooper is foolish to keep antagonizing the people of the town. To the surprise of everyone, Hooper proves he is right and comes up with a murderer. The story has an unexpected ending but is not exciting reading. Only fair. (M. Broset)

THE DOCUMENTS IN THE CASE
(Letters)

From Ellen Nehr, 207 S. Cassidy Rd., Bexley, OH 43209:
I hereby certify that I have met Martin M. Wooster and that
he is alive and breathing the air of Beloit, Wisconsin. The
question which was raised as to whether or not he is "for
real" is much too complex for me to even attempt to answer.
Have you invented a character in order to beef up "The Documents in the Case"? Of course you have, and I'm just surprised that no one has called you on it earlier. Jeff Banks
has to be an alter ego who says the things that you want to
say but feel will come better from an outsider. Point one:
he hides behind a post office box. Point two: even Rand-McNally can't find Nacodgoches, Texas. It must be an anagram
for some esoteric prairie bird. Point three: he HATES letters of comment and takes every opportunity to tell you and
us so in a thousand or more well chosen words which always
make each issue come out to the exact number of pages you
have planned. Point four: he started this male/female argument which ended up with you losing a subscriber from Sweden.
Now that you have the character, I can't wait to read the
plot. ¶ Despite all the hot air currently floating around
Ohio during this election campaign, winter is just about here
and I have been getting organized to write the final definitive article on a subject dear to my heart which should start
your Volume 3 off with more than even your usual touch of
class. "Little Old Ladies Which (That) I Have Known and
Loved" will include hats, cats, knitting bags, pictures of
the grandchildren and all sorts of other favorite things.
Just think--when it is done the subject then will be closed
and you won't have to worry about them cluttering up your
pristine pages again. Please note that I didn't once mention Bouchercon and the Hula you did in the lobby at 3 a.m.
Oh, you will publish LOLs without any editorial comment? I
thought you might see it my way. [*It wasn't the Hula; it
was the Charleston, as you would have seen if you hadn't had
that silly lamp shade over your head. Please note that I
didn't once mention what else you were wearing. Or were not
wearing.*]

From Jon L. Breen, 10642 La Bahia Ave., Fountain Valley, CA:
Thanks for another lively issue. George Kelley says in his
Bill Pronzini article, "A Korean War veteran, Pronzini has
Connell karating people left and right." Bill Pronzini is
about my age and not old enough to be a Korean War veteran.
¶ Yes, I was able to figure out that the sentence meant that
Connell was a Korean War veteran, but George Kelley should
pay heed to the following grammatical rule, stated by Stephen
Goldin in the Science Fiction Writers of America *Bulletin*:
"When dangling, don't use participles." Or, my rule, more
relevant to this instance: "Easily misplaced, you should
closely guard your modifiers."

From Jeff Banks, Box 3007 SFA Sta., Nacogdoches, TX 75962:
Your latest issue was enough late that I was beginning to
worry (probably because MFr has been so dependably on time
in the past), but I can certainly pronounce it well worth
waiting for. One more enamored of the pun than I (and you'd

have to search long and hard for such a person) might say it somehow seemed fancier than ever before. ¶ The new duplication system seems to have levelled out near perfection. The cover is a delight, and I hope you are going to run sketches of other well-known 'tec' writers--I wouldn't want you to stop the other sort of covers, but an author cover about once out of every three issues would be very nice. ¶ I especially enjoyed the Kelley article on Pronzini (who has to rank near the top of the "unfairly underrated mystery writers"), and I was glad to see the article and reviews by Marty Wooster. Perhaps he was just a shade less acerbic, but it may just be that he found the materials treated this time more acceptable. ¶ Steve covered 27 books, but only two of them p.i. books, both of which I had already seen. Yet, I found several special pleasures in his column anyway. I had read that "Mike Roscoe" book so long ago that I'd forgotten how much I enjoyed it (and how much better I think it is than the contemporary book Steve mentions in connection with it); his (Steve's) treatment was perfect for this book, quoting plenty to give the "flavor"--and that is always the main thing a parody has going for it. Also, I was pleased to see him saluting the overlap between Mystery and Western fiction. I know Steve is interested particularly in that fairly frequent blend, as he and I have corresponded regarding it in relation to my "Mystery +" column in *The Poisoned Pen*. Finally, I found about the usual amount of disagreement with his taste on several particular books, but that is a large part of the fun of knowing a critic well. Thanks to your publication, more and more mystery fans are getting to know Steve well as a critic; I say (as I've said before) that he is one of the best. ¶ The total of 24 miscellaneous reviews was also a delight. But what a disappointment that not a one of them was a p.i. book. I hope all of your reviewers aren't saving their reactions to p.i. books to appear in Andy Jaysnovitch's new magazine *The Not So Private Eye*. It's a delight to have a publication devoted exclusively to my most favorite kind of reading, but I'd hate to see coverage of the eye books dropped by all the other 'zines.

From Bill Crider, 4206 Ninth Street, Brownwood, TX 76801:
I came in from school today to discover that TMF had arrived; so I sat down and read it from cover to cover. I have a few comments, and I think I'll start with the cover. I liked it, but it aroused false hopes. I thought there would be, inside, an article on the strangely neglected Ken Crossen, creator of Milo March and other well-oiled private eyes. Alas, there was no such article. Maybe I can stir up a little interest with a trivia question: Was Crossen the first writer to use the drug LSD as a major plot device? I am willing to bet that he was. (See *The Splintered Man*, published under the name of M. E. Chaber, Rinehart, 1955; Perma, 1957.) ¶ If Stephen Mertz likes your typos, he must love the fact that you confused his letter with one by Jeff Banks (or vice-versa) [*picky, picky, picky*] in "Mysteriously Speaking . . .". And Martin Wooster, if he really exists (and I have to believe that he does; you couldn't possibly be doing his fanzine for DAPA-EM), must really be agog that you transposed two pages of his article, especially considering some of your comments about him in the past. [*You know, Bill, I'd really like to see your collection of nits someday.*] Of Coarse, as you are awear, I never meke mesteakes myselve.
¶ I don't often see reviews of Richard Neely's work, but

Steve Lewis had comments on two of Neeley's books. I've just finished *No Certain Life*, and I want to add a little to what Steve said. It's certainly true that Neely doesn't "play fair" in this book. It seems to me that he does books like this one quite often, though, and that this particular story wasn't written just with the movies in mind. By "books like this one," I mean books that, in the last fifty pages or so, have twist after twist after twist, until nothing is as it had appeared to be. *The Walter Syndrome* and *The Japanese Misteress* come to mind immediately, and there've been a number of others. Playing fair doesn't mean a thing: Neely is interested in surprising you, and he delivers. Steve was scrupulous about not revealing the plot of *No Certain Life*, but I think it's fair to say that the twists don't let up until the very last sentence, which contains a final turn of the screw (there's a good phrase, Henry, write it down) that no movie will be able to duplicate. For those who like this sort of plotting, Neely is hard to beat. ¶ At the risk of being crude, and I'm a notably unrefined person, I've got to take issue with the abbreviation for TMF that Jeff Banks uses in his letter. Somehow, I can't read MFr without getting the wrong idea. Probably just my vulgarity, and I beg your pardon, Jeff; I'm sure that no one even knows what I'm talking about, unless you have a subscriber by the name of Oedipus. [*Oeditor's note: Er, I'm glad you mentioned this, Bill; for the longest time I thought mine was the only crude and vulgar mind to make the connection. It's comforting to know that I'm not alone in my crudeness and vulgarity. In addition to being crude and vulgar, my mind is also sometimes suspicious, and I have suspected all along that Jeff's choice of those particular initials was quite deliberate.*] ¶ Moving right along (feel free to censor the above paragraph; you know how off-the-wall my writing is [*I know, but I've got to fill these pages somehow . . .*]), I have to say to Marv Lachman, whose work I've enjoyed in TAD as well as TMF, ane even in the old TMRN, that I don't agree that there would be no articles for such publications as those referred to if books like *The Hanged Men* were the rule. Lots of people liked *The Hanged Men*. I did, anyway. But I'd probably never bother to read *Darkness at Pemberley*. Nevertheless, I do a fanzine for DAPA-EM, I write you letters, I send you reviews, and I generally have a good time. Marv may think that I'm all wet, but then I think he just may be missing the boat on Spillane, too. And I guess all that's part of the fun.

From Mitchell Grand, 2345 N. Second St., Harrisburg, PA: Although this is my first letter to you, I'm not going to tell you how much I like TMF until I get something off my chest. ¶ And it all comes from reading your "Mysteriously Speaking". You speak of manners and good taste and the lack of respect in the country today. ¶ I don't know if you read *Bookviews*--a monthly on books published by R. R. Bowker Company. (They published Hagan's book on mystery fiction.) The October issue has William F. Buckley, Jr., on the cover and an article about him inside. ¶ William F. Buckley, Jr., has written two thrillers, *Saving the Queen* and *Stained Glass*. He's been lucky enough to have had them on the Best Seller list. Evidently he feels this entitles him to sound off on one of the greats, Agatha Christie! ¶ In the article he writes--"If I read something badly written it troubles me. I can't, for example, read a book of Agatha Christie's--I keep gagging." ¶ In the same paragraph he writes "But I couldn't read a biography of me" by Agatha Christie. ¶ In your editorial you write, "I do not say that sarcasm and ridicule should never be used; but I do say that they can honorably be used only as defensive, not offensive weapons." ¶ Buckley shows a lack of good taste, manners and respect! Mostly respect! ¶ He probably doesn't care that Christie has brought joy and happiness to more readers than any other writer including the Bard of Avon. ¶ When I'm feeling low, there are only two writers I can read--Christie and Simenon. I don't agree with everything that Christie writes. I don't like her ethnic slurs, especially those written under the name of Mary Westmacott. ¶ But surely her surprise endings are in a class by themselves. ¶ Maybe Buckley wanted to join the literary greats Edmund Wilson and Robert Coates--who also dislike Christie. ¶ But that word "gagging"! "No respect," as Rodney Dangerfield would say. Perhaps the Mystery Writers of America and the Crime Writers Association of England could punish him in some way. Enough. [*Buckley is a reactionary ass; unfortunately, he is also quite brilliant.*] ¶ Now to TMF. I now have every issue but volume 1, #1. All great--but vol. 2, #5 is simply in a class by itself! After reading it last night I felt a glow after your last paragraph--"You are good folks, every damned one of you." ¶ Where else would you find the editor of *The Poisoned Pen*--Jeff Meyerson--writing a letter praising TMF! And vice versa. ¶ And Steve Lewis is the best. And I've gotten some fine books from his lists. ¶ I don't agree with everything George Kelley says about Bill Pronzini. To paraphrase the late Will Rogers, "I never read a Bill Pronzini I didn't like." ¶ After reading Marvin Lachman's "It's About Crime" I'm sorry Dover stopped sending me their lists. I'd surely have ordered *Darkness at Pemberley* by T. H. White. ¶ This letter's getting too long--and I'll just say I like everything about TMF. And you can count on me as a fulltime subscriber. Oh yes, I enjoyed Dick Moskowitz's letter.

From Michael Doran, 4117 W. 90th Place, Hometown, IL 60456: Your September-October issue arrived, fittingly, on November first. Everything is late this month for some reason. The November and December EQMM's went on sale here in Chicago within a week of each other. I'll try not to see any significance in this. ¶ I have read and reread Martin Wooster's letter in 2:5, and I'm prepared to admit he may be on to something with regard to the later Ellery Queen novels. I have two reservations to express: 1) Since Wooster does not (overtly) dispute the participation of Frederic Dannay in these books, he is misusing the term "ghost-written" to describe them. Personnel changes within a collaboration are not unheard of in mystery fiction (see under "Patrick Quentin"). In the EQ stories, the plots (Dannay's plots, by Wooster's admission) are the main attraction, so "authenticity" is not the issue. (My opinion.) 2) Wooster's speculation as to why Manfred Lee was not involved in these books is just a bit too flip and facile to suit me. "Burned out" can mean any of a dozen different things. Documentation of some sort is required; otherwise, all Wooster's statement becomes is a *National Enquirer*-style cheap shot. Until and unless Wooster provides us with *facts*, about Lee and about the collaborators, both remain in the realm of unsubstantiated rumor. The bothersome part of this is that Wooster is an excellent writer, and a sharp critic; the insults are gratuitous and unnecessary, as is the gossip. (I just read all of the foregoing over again and shocked myself with how intense I am about this. As an explanation, I humbly submit that my daily exposure to Chicago's own king of search-and-destroy journalism, Gary Deeb of the *Tribune*, has given me a very low opinion of semi-factual reporting. I'm starting to rant--better leave this part out. The stuff in parentheses, I mean. [*Okay*.]) ¶ This may interest Mike Nevins: I found his new novel, *Corrupt and Ensnare*, in the general fiction section, not among the mysteries. The jacket blurb doesn't hide the fact that the book is a mystery, but doesn't proclaim it either. His idea, or Putnam's? And while I think of it, in his guest editorial in the most recent TAD, Nevins refers to having seen the Nero Wolfe telefilm. Since ABC has *never* televised the film, I'd love to know where and when he saw it. (Trust me that it hasn't been on the air--network television is one of the few professional sports I follow. If the N.W. movie had been shown, I'd know about it.) ¶ [...] One last dumb question: Were you leveling when you described yourself as a short fat guy with frizzy hair and a beard? "Guy Townsend" sounds like a character from an Errol Flynn movie. Sorry about that. I fell into the habit long ago of casting actors in the stories I read, and when physical descriptions aren't provided, I go by the names. Now I find myself doing it with nonfiction writers when their publishers don't put pictures on the jacket. I'd appreciate it if some other TMFer would admit to doing this too, just so I'd know I'm not the only nut who does it. [*You are quite right, Mike; I do look like Errol Flynn.*]

From Thomas L. Motsinger, Rt. 1, Box 759, Colfax, NC 27235: I have just completed reading the five TMF's you sent me on this year's subscription and have enjoyed them immensely, even more than the other fan magazines to which I subscribe. I especially enjoy the review columns and I have attempted to write one myself, the first time I have ever attempted to write for a fan magazine. I hope you can use it in a future TMF. ¶ In the future issues of TMF, I hope you can have some articles on my favorite detective and author, Ellery Queen.

From Joe Lansdale, Rt. 8, Box 231, Nacogdoches, TX 75961: Thank you for the latest TMF. I enjoyed it. Found the material on Uncle Abner interesting and the article on Bill Pronzini gave me the names of some new books to look up. I think Bill's best work is by far his private eye novels, *Undercurrent* probably geing the very best, but all others sliding in close. Personally, I prefer *Games* to *Snowbound*, but with two fine books like that it's hard to choose one over the other. Maybe my preference for *Games* is my recent reading of it. ¶ One thing threw me. Your editorial singles out Jeff Bank's letter and says, "Jeff seems to imply what I know he does not believe, that Manners and Good Taste are not compatible with Honesty." ¶ I reread friend Jeff's letter three times looking for that implication. Where did you find it? Did Jeff write another letter, perhaps unpublished? Did that sneaking devil use disappearing ink? Or perhaps he has the power to cloud men's minds, and while mine was clouded through three readings I missed the subtleties of his suggestion. But clouding minds through paper? Not even the Shadow has such skill. However, strange are the ways of University professors. [*What a sarcastic gastard you are, Joe. Obviously, I meant to say Steve Mertz rather than Jeff Banks. I've been trying to figure out how I could have made so gross an error, but all I've been able to come up with is this: I am so used to Jeff's wrong-headed remarks about Spillane and letters of comment that the wrong-headedness of Steve's Good Taste remarks subconsciously triggered Jeff's name in my mind as I typed up my remarks in the last issue. How's that for spreading oil on troubled waters? A little poke in the eye for everyone. Seriously, though, I do apologize to Jeff for taking his name in vain.*] ¶ Whatever, the whole thing about Wooster is silly and I'll let it rest. ¶ Hope the little collaboration by Jeff and Harry Dawson leads to more. I think maybe you could sucker Dawson into your ranks. I took a spy class taught by Dawson and Banks and it was a lot of fun. I'm not ordinarily a spy fan, but they used a good choice of books and approached it with James Bondish enthusiasm. ¶ As always, the reviews were nice and the letters were fun. Perhaps, if I can manage the extra time from my fledgling attempts to write stories and maintain my janitorial duties at the University here, I'll send along a book review myself. ¶ If you feel up to a bit of self torture, watch for my forthcoming second sale, "Long Gone, Forever", scheduled for the December issue of *Mike Shayne*. ¶ Whoops! One more thing. ¶ Patricia Parnell, Batman is too a detective. (Sound of tongue making rude noise.) So there! If not for *Batman* and *Detective* comics at a very tender age, I might never have become interested in detective fiction. I think he's the basis for my being such a private eye fan. The lone vigilante sort out to right wrongs and all that. Good fantasy stuff. True, Robin was a klutz from time to time and I always wondered how a kid in a green, red and yellow costume managed to sneak up on so many badies, and why didn't those funny looking little elf shoes come off. Huh! Somebody out there answer that! (No comments from Dick Grayson, please.) ¶ And while we're on it, will nobody stand up for Modesty and Nick? ¶ In all honesty, I do feel Penzler missed out on a few goodies, Pronzini and the Prather books for instance, but wasted paper on Batman! How dare you, Pat.. Next you'll be saying there is no Doc Savage.

From Jeff Meyerson, 50 First Place, Brokly, NY 11231:
I enjoyed the latest issue of *FANcier*, even though it was a bit difficult to read in spots. I'm sure once you're more used to your new equipment that will clear up. As much as I enjoy the writings of Jeff Banks (and that's very much indeed), I disagree totally on his ideas of the best makeup of a successful fanzine. I like as many letters as possible, Jeff's near the top of the list. I find that with Steve's excellent review column and the other review section, it makes too much of a block to read all at once. I need something to break up all those reviews and for me, that is the letter column. This issue's column is a perfect example. First off, I must apologize to Steve Mertz for making perhaps a too hasty judgment on Carroll John Daly. I will attempt to find and read some of his other works before passing final judgment. Steve is certainly right about the inanity of most publishers. I did notice, however, that one of Daly's books was on sale at Bouchercon in a new large format paperback

48

printing. Sorry, but I don't remember which it was. Another interesting fact about Daly that Steve might not know: at least two of his books were published in British paperback in the thirties in the Hutchinson Crime Book Society series. This series seems to have been mostly British thriller writers like Wallace, Horler and the like, though they also did an Old Man in the Corner collection (#4 *Unravelled Knots*), Eden Phillpotts' *Found Drowned* (#7--plus others by Phillpotts), and several by Anthony Wynne, among others. The two by Daly were *Murder Won't Wait* (#70) and *The Amateur Murderer* (#79). I hope to have a complete checklist in a future *Pen*. ¶ My favorite letter was John Nieminski's on the "existence" of Martin Wooster. I guess John's question about whether or not he is real was answered in Chicago (or was it?). Martin's own letter made me quite angry, though not at him specifically. So Sturgeon "admitted to writing *The Player on the Other Side*" did he? Isn't that nice? Perhaps he was playing on Martin's naivete, but if he is seriously handing out garbage like that he ought to watch his step. It reminds me of a guy we observed on a bus in London this summer who "wrote" "Nobody Does It Better" and a few other songs which were "stolen" from him by famous artists. Of course he was just out of the loony bin . . . . ¶ Jeff Banks' letter reminds me that someone at the convention, in trying to recall the name of the Memphis paper, came up with a great one--*The Memphis Pi(d)geon Fancier*! I know that isn't its name, but maybe it should be. Normally I read the letters first, but this time I disciplined myself and forced myself to wait till the end. Keep the column as big and lively as it is now, please! ¶ The rest of the mag, George, Marv, etc. were up to the usual fine standards, and I hope there will indeed continue to be those interesting chart articles. Keep it up.

From Joe Hensley, 2315 Blackmore, Madison, IN 47250:
I was through Memphis Friday night and stayed in a motel (Quality Inn East, I think). Wish I'd had Vol. 2 # 5 then as I'd have called. But I'll be there again the middle of June of 1979 and perhaps will call you then. [*Okay. HENCEFORTH, I would appreciate it if people who stop at or pass through Memphis without giving me a call would refrain from mentioning it to me later. My teeth can't take much more gnashing.*] [. . .] ¶ 2/5 was interesting, particularly the reviews and letters. I make lists of books I've missed which draw enthusiastic reviews and try to find them either in the library or in paper. So I appreciate the grading, even though I don't always agree with it. ¶ I'm glad you've decided to let Martin Wooster go on. But you really don't need me to help conduct your defense--what you need is to try it in my court. ¶ I've ordered Mike's new book and hope it comes along soon. Things are slow for me these days because of a rather exhausting trial schedule. I've another starting tomorrow, this one an attempted murder. I tried a three week long murder case in Sept./Oct. and have a couple more that I must move along. But I have sold another Robak novel to the Crime Club (not yet completed) and *A Killing in Gold* has been picked up by Gallancz in England. I've even done some short things, the first in years. There's one in the current issue of *Galileo*, a collaboration with Gene DeWeese. It's science fiction, but we've also done a suspense thing, which may work out, and I've done a couple of other things on my own. ¶ Thanks for TMF. I found myself ignor-

ing things that needed doing until I'd finished it.

From Mary A. Seeger, 6977 Alaska Ave. S.E., Caledonia, MI:
I enjoyed meeting you at Bouchercon IX. . . . As I promised, here are the tables of contents of the latest issues of the Swedish mags *Jury* and *Dast*. ¶ *Jury*, now in its seventh year, is a quarterly, now appearing as a paperback book. Subscription price 45 Swedish crowns. The current issue, 3/78, 82 pp., begins with a list of every new Swedish detective and thriller novel (48), then a list of the ± 150 translated into Swedish; then collections and anthologies; critical lit. and finally book club offerings. The articles in the journal itself: Another good detective year! (editor's summary of the crime scene); Meeting with Hammond Innes (interview conducted by Jan Broberg, one of Sweden's best critics and anthologists); The myth of the huge printings of detective novels (a lament that there aren't larger printings); The sliced mollusk, or the detective novel in 1000 morsels (review of critical lit.); Interview with Kennet Ahl (Swedish author); The evil, the good, and the passive (the novels of Hans Hellmut Kirst); Plus there's lots more--limericks; reviews; Broberg's continuing column; a report on the crime scene in London, etc. *Jury* welcomes contributions; has no letters column. If you'd like anything translated, Guy, we'd need the editor's permission, but I've corresponded with him, so that's probably no problem. [*Regarding translations, I'm sure I speak for a good many TMFers when I say that I'd be delighted to know what's going on in Scandinavia, but, since you are the one who knows the language, and what's in each article, it would be silly for me to try to tell you which ones to translate for TMF. Why don't you just pick out a goodie from time to time and send it to me? And while I'm at it, I hope you will continue to do these tables of contents rundowns for TMF.*] ¶ *Dast* is celebrating its tenth anniversary, and the slick photo cover features the Nicaraguan Interpol stamps of the fictional detective, in color, no less. This is issue 72 (Vol. XI, Nr. 5). Costs 40 Swedish crowns for 6 issues in a year. Pages--56 in this issue. Included are: Review of Fanzines, including TMF; Reviews. News of Norwegian and French books; Letters; Interview with Alfred Coppel; Science fiction corner; List of SF/thriller/detective fiction that has appeared in *Playboy*; Article on Agatha Christie by la Cour (*Murder Book*); Continuing biblio of the works of Sven Elvestad; Article in English by Geoffrey Jenkins on his own works. [. . .] ¶ Let me know how I might be a link with the Scandinavian and German scenes. I've translations of lots of Broberg's stuff that TAD has not published, and some of them might interest you. [*Send 'em on.*]

From Martin Morse Wooster, Box 1691 Beloit College, Beloit, WI:
I have had many accusations thrust against me in mystery fandom, but never of being a pseudonym. My talks with Nieminski at Bouchercon should have proved to his satisfaction that I do indeed exist, and am not a figment of your wily imagination. After all, it's very easy to find books at the Library of Congress--all you need is a stack pass . . . . ¶ Michael Doran and Marvin Lachman both accuse me of rumor-mongering. I cheerfully admit to it. I've proved that at least one book attributed to Queen was not, in fact, written by them. As for the remainder of Queen's work, I honestly don't know who wrote what. I strongly suspect that Dannay and Lee farmed

out contracts, but cannot prove it. I do feel a duty to put the rumors on record, so that those who do know can either prove or disprove them. Lachman, though, takes the sanctity of the Queen pseudonym to extremes; surely he does not believe that the Tim Corrigan books were turned out by Dannay and Lee? Even Al Hubin, in his checklist of series characters, puts the authorship of this series in quotations--"Ellery Queen". (I've since heard, by the way, that two of the Tim Corrigan books were written by Jack Vance. Apparently all the authors of this series were clients of Scott Meredith, and he was throwing the contracts to anyone who walked in the door--in a figurative, *not* literal sense.) ¶ I don't see why people should complain horribly about your upping your subscription rates 15%. TAD just upped its rates 60%--and not only gave no information as to why the increase occurred, but gave no warning to its subscribers. Compared to this shoddy conduct, your announcements are honorable--I only hope that stalwart contributors can subscribe at the old rates . . . (We do, after all, pay for *information*, not for neato pictures or cute letterheads.) ¶ And speaking of conspiracies--*why* did you switch two pages of my review? I'm both honored and surprised to have an article in the September/October issue, but I do wish you would get the pages ordered correctly. [*I did not* consciously *get your pages out of order. Seeing as how it was your article alone which was disordered, though, I don't deny that my subconscious may have had a hand in it.*] ¶ Tell Jeff Banks and his friends to keep turning out those spy charts. Banks is right--the chart *is* a useful way to compress information into a small space. I only hope that you can print his Joe Gall chart soon. What next--Sam Durell?

From Perry C. Dillon, 2009 N.W. 29th, Okalhoma City, OK: I am like several of your readers, whose letters I read with glee--that is, one who is not a collector, but who would like to be; one who doesn't know all the authors being discussed, but who would like to; etc. So, I read the reviews and letters in growing amazement, yet enjoyed every minute. ¶ I love the informal style of the "zine" (a new word for me), the mutterings about British spellings, the misplacements of quotation marks (in front of commas, for example)--and I say, don't change a damned thing: it is a *terrific* "zine." [*As a courtesy, I have refrained from altering the arrangement of Perry's punctuation on the two occasions in this letter when he ends a sentence with "zine." But see my remarks below.*] ¶ But as to Vol. 2, No. 5, which is what has really prompted this outpouring. First, kudos to Marvin Lachman for his comments on *The Hanged Men*! After reading several glowing reviews of that book, I wondered whether I had read the same book as the reviewers. Marvin Lachman says exactly what I felt about that work: it was "fast-moving . . . , readable but forgettable," although I might add (as he implies in his later remarks) that it is not "forgettable" in the sense that it infuriates in its depiction of contemporary "with-itness" (my stupid word, not Mr. Lachman's). Such retrospective reviews are very important, I feel. Praise be to Marvin Lachman! ¶ Among the many other fine reviews in TMF, I feel that I have to comment on Steve Lewis' review of Janwillem van de Wetering's *The Japanese Corpse*. I enjoy all of Mr. Lewis' reviews, and this one I certainly felt superior (*superior* to other people's reviews, not to his, all of which are

superior). In trying to summarize this book to a fellow
adict whom I wanted to read it, I found myself fumbling and
stumbling for words, finally ending up saying something like:
"Well, this novel is like most great novels: it just can't be
summarized." Sure, that statement was true, but I was also
using it to cop-out. Then I read in Steve Lewis' review:
"The climax is an explosive celebration of friendship and
justice between men, between East and West, between even good
and evil." Why couldn't I have said that? His whole last
paragraph was one of the finest examples of what (I feel) reviewers ought to be saying about books. ¶ And finally, I
have one small quibble, concerning Amnon Kabatchnik's review
of Simenon's *Maigret and the Hotel Majestic*. Having only
read the first five issues of Vol. 2, I had wondered where
reviews of Simenon's books were, whether your readers were
even reading Simenon. Surely *Maigret and the Hotel Majestic*
is not an introduction of "the American public to Simenon's
art and Maigret's humanity"? If so, what a pity, for this
work, though interesting as Simenon's consistently are, is
not one of his best, nor is it the best introduction to Maigret. Many of the Maigret series have been out in English
translation for some time. Why aren't they being reviewed?
¶ While I find Mr. Kabatchnik's review of *Maigret and the
Hotel Majestic* a good review, evenly balanced and fair, I do
object to the old cliché about Maigret: that he "displays no
conspicuous physical or intellectual gifts and boasts no
striking personal eccentricities. He is a very ordinary man,
domestic, almost dull. . . ." Sure, he's no idiosyncratic
Dr. Fell or S. Holmes, but what a character! Full of humanity, kindliness, love for the wretched of this earth; a fair,
amiable man, seldom provoked to violence; a quiet, thoughtful
man, one who, as Kabatchnik says, "tries to re-live the psy-
chological crisis which triggered the crime and understand
the warped humanity from which criminal impulses emerge."
In this day of Enforcers and secret agents, how idiosyncratic
this Maigret is when he tries to understand rather than to
maim and kill! ¶ Enough ravings! Many best wishes for continued successes with your excellent "zine." [*I hold the
University of Chicago* **Manual of Style** *in very high esteem and
bow to it at almost every turn, largely because the stands it
takes are for the most part logical. One of the very few
things over which I take exception with it is the matter of
enclosing commas within quotation marks. Quotation marks are
supposed to enclose quoted material or certain types of titles. There are other uses to which they are put, but these
are their principal applications. If a question mark is a
part of a quote or a title, it should be enclosed within the
marks; if it is not--e.g.* **Have you seen** *"The Mousetrap"? or* **Did you
hear him say** *"I am guilty"?--it should be outside the marks. On
this the* **Manual of Style** *and I agree. Logically, commas should
be treated the same way. I won't go into an extended argument regarding commas in quotations (though logic favors*
"What the hell", *Smith bellowed,* "do you think you are doing?" *over*
"What the hell," *Smith bellowed,* "do you think you are doing?" *if only
because what Smith actually bellowed was* "What the hell do you
think you are doing?" *rather than* "What the hell, do you think you are
doing?"*), but I will take this opportunity to rail against the
illogical and stupid practice of enclosing commas in quotation marks around titles or, for that matter, any word or
short phrase that is enclosed in quotation marks for emphasis.
The title of Dame Agatha's play is* "The Mousetrap", *not* "The

Mousetrap Comma", and anyone who wants to argue differently may find the pedants on his side but logic--and I--will be against him. And where, I would dearly like to know, is the logic behind enclosing periods within quotation marks, unless one is quoting a complete, declarative sentence? The corrupt word for publications such as TMF is "zine", not "zine," or "zine." or "zine?" or "zine;" or "zine:" or "zine!". Just "zine!". Period.]

From Gerie Frazier, 415 Sage Hill St. Apt B, Rawlins, WY:
So glad you received our change of address in time for mailing TMF 2:5 which arrived October 16th. GREAT COVER!! Hope the talented ones out there will keep you well supplied with cover art in future. ¶ Thanks for letting us know of the reason for the delay in getting the second class mailing permit--that is hilarious. ¶ Another fine issue of TMF. I particularly enjoyed "Bill Pronzini Revisited" by George Kelley, as I have read quite a few of Pronzini's short stories published in mystery magazines and am somewhat of a fan of his. I was interested to learn that Mr. P. has written other material under pseudonyms, but the "shocker" was in reading that *The Jade Figurine* was published in 1972 as a novel under the pseudonym "Jack Foxx". ¶ I had just recently reread *The Jade Figurine*, by *Bill Pronzini*, published as a novelette in the January, 1971, issue of AHMM. In that, Dan Connell's partner was Lawrence Falco (not Pete), and La Croix's partner was Tina Kellogg. The name "Maria King" does not appear in the novelette. In reading it, I found it to be very well written, fast paced and the characters quite well defined. Hope the local library has the 1972 (Bobbs-Merrill) book by "Jack Foxx" so that I can read it and compare. ¶ George Kelley's comments on *Freebooty* also "rang a bell". It has been a few years since I read that, and it is currently not accessible to me, being in storage. However, I am quite sure that this story also appeared in either AHMM or EQMM some time back, as a novelette. Not being blessed with total recall, I can't remember if the story was published under that exact title, and whether or not Bill Pronzini was listed as the author. The only way I could be sure the novelette I read is the same as *Freebooty* would be if George had written a slightly longer review of it and had made some mention of "Pinkerton agents!". ¶ I am glad to have learned something new (to me) about Pronzini from this article, and if George Kelley is unaware of the foregoing, I hope it may be of some interest to him. ¶ Your Nero Wolfe Saga is "tops" as usual, and the letters section quite enjoyable . . . as Dick Moskowitz wrote: "just one big happy family--although scattered around the world".

From Bob Briney, 4 Forest Ave., Salem, MA 01970:
The latest TMF was just the right length to fit the plane trip [back from Bouchercon], or vice versa. (Four hours door-to-door, of which an hour and a half were actually spent in the air.) Topping off the weekend with comments on the magazine seems somehow appropriate, and it will also clear the decks for all the non-mystery work that has to be done tomorrow. ¶ Following the pattern of Martin Wooster's reviews of the Mystery Library volumes, I have to give TMF 2:5 a double rating: contents, A, as usual; printing, C+. That is, of course, highly unfair, since the printing job is really impressive for a first encounter with an offset press.

But there were those pages on which I had to deduce the first several letters of each line. . . . ¶ At the top of this issue's contents, I would have to put John Nieminski's letter, closely followed by Steve's reviews and the current installment of the Saga. ¶ I know what John means about leaving 40% of new mysteries unfinished. When I left for Chicago on Friday, I was nearly halfway through Elizabeth Foote-Smith's *Never Say Die*. Seeing it on the kitchen table when I got back this evening, I realized that I couldn't remember much of anything about the characters or the plot, and had no great desire to refresh my memory. Perhaps I'll change my mind when the delights of the weekend have faded somewhat, but at the moment the temptation is to consign the book to the discard pile. ¶ Hope you found someone to do a full writeup on Bouchercon. With lots of photos. It was a great weekend. I especially appreciated the chance to meet you, and trust It won't be the last time. [*Same here, Bob.*] ¶ P.S.: Is there any special reason for Ken Crossen's portrait to be on the cover of TMF, when he is not even mentioned anywhere inside the issue? In this rendering, he looks a great deal like sf writer Harry Harrison. [*As you know, TMF is chronically short on cover art, and I use whatever I can get, whenever I can get it, especially when it's something super like Frank Hamilton's covers. I would like to be able to hold on to art until I have an article to match, but it just isn't possible so long as I am averaging something less than one cover contribution per issue. I'm glad you mentioned this, though, because it gives me an opportuntity to apologize to Frank for not crediting him inside. I don't think he has ever really forgiven me for the slighting remarks I made about artwork in fanzines in the Preview Issue of TMF, and now I've gone and rubbed salt in the wound by not even acknowledging that he is the creator of the best TMF cover yet. Sorry, Frank. Forgive me?*]

From David H. Doerrer, 4626 Baywood Circle, Pensacola, FL: I was tremendously impressed at meeting you at Bouchercon 9. Truly, you are a master of disguise. I would never have guessed that your normal appearance is that of a "short, fat fellow with frizzy red hair, a full flowing beard and a squint." Just think, if you had gotten TMF 2:5 out on schedule a lot of readers might have thought you were being impersonated! ¶ I know that you will have a report of Bouchercon 9 from someone (though I can't remember who at the moment), so I won!t attempt to add anything to that save a few comments on my own personal reactions. I enmoyed every minute of it! As good as the program was, I think I got even more out of the opportunity to match faces and personalities with the names of fans and authors whom I've gotten to know through their writings. My one regret is at having so little time to talk with many of you. ¶ Which leads me into my first comment on TMF in this letter. Don't shorten the letter column! I think the letters even more than the contributions make TMF a magazine by and for fans. I don't say you shouldn't edit, for that is a decision you should remain free to make for yourself. I also realize that a time may well come when you might have to both select which letters you publish and also edit those you select for length in order to keep an issue (or issues) from being more letters than anything else, but I don't think a quarter or less of a 60+

page issue to much to devote to letters. Once again, I have to use Jeff Banks' letter in 2:5 as one in point. I wouldn't have wanted to have any of it cut, despite Jeff's own suggestion that it could have been. Enough on what seems to be becoming one of *my* hobby horses. ¶ Thanks to my own dilatory habits, I once again have two issues to comment on. Since one item occurs in both, I'll tackle that first; which I should preface by saying that I met and talked with Martin Wooster at Bouchercon 9. Neither of us mentioned the controversy over his reviews, although Martin did indicate that he was distressed that some people felt he didn't exist. Having both 2:4 and 2:5 in hand as I write this, my perspective is a bit different than it might have been earlier. As it is, I agree with you, Guy, in your reappraisal of the propriety of your taking Martin to task in the editorial column. As several people pointed out in the letters in 2:5, if he has discovered factual errors as he reports, whoever was responsible deserves to be called for them. On the other hand, if *he* is in error, then someone is also going to call him to account. I'm not sure the vehemence is necessary or adds anything to the criticism, but if that is a part of Martin's style, I can read it for what it is, no more, no less. I was fortunate enough to meet John Nieminski at Bouchercon 9 (James Ullman introduced me to him) but before I had read his letter in 2:5 so I don't know if he was serious or tongue-in-cheek about your perpetrating a "hoax". Of his experiences at the Library of Congress versus Martin's ability to provide bibliographic services, Martin works there, and we all know that an inside man always has an edge. Seriously, though, I visited LC in 1969 and toured their Loan and Stack Division. Conditions were just plain awful. As a then young librarian, I was appalled at being told that they had no search mechanism for "not-on-shelf" books, i.e. if it wasn't there the requestor was just told to try again. Since Daniel Boorstin took over as Librarian of Congress, they have been studying some of their internal problems (among other things) and the *Library of Congress Information Bulletin* has carried a couple of articles on their analysis of "not-on-shelf" problems. However, since John was there recently, they obviously haven't progressed beyond the study stage. My point here is: if the services Martin offers would help you, take him up on his offer. His work on "Maarten Maartens" demonstrates that he has both the ability and the resources available to do a sound bit of bibliographic research. ¶ Well, maybe Jeff has a point. This letter is looking like getting longer yet already than I think when I start. (You don't really mean that you prefer literate and grammatical contributions, do you, Guy?) ¶ Guy, a loud and heart-felt "Amen" to your sentiments on the importance of Manners and Good Taste in a civilized society! I could go on at considerable length about how right you are, but then this is the MYSTERY FANcier and not something else, so I won't. I will offer a couple of quotations which I think are apropos: "Unhappily, the demand for equal treatment generally takes the form of equal immunity for all, rather than equal subjection to rational regulation for all."--Richard W. Lyman, President of Stanford University in an address to the 78th meeting of the Association of Research Libraries, Colorado Springs, May 14-15, 1971. "Your freedom to swing your arm ends where my nose starts."-- Unknown. ¶ All right. Enough. A page and a half down and what do I have to say about TMF 2:4 and 2:5? Too much. Each issue keeps getting better and better. Much of what I could say has been said, at least about 2:4, already, so I'll hit highlights in short sentences rather than my usual long-winded paragraphs. (My wife has been telling me for years that my style is too verbose.) ¶ TMF 2:4--Thanks to George Kelley I'll try another Tony Kenrick and see if I like him better when he emphasizes "humor over plot". I thought you might get someone carping over the lengthy quotations in Jane S. Bakerman's fine analytical article; glad you didn't. Kudos to Theodore P. Dukeshire for giving me other Mike Lockens to look for. Even the movie they made of *The Killer Elite* wasn't too bad, allowing for the major changes in character, plot, climax, ending, etc.! Ditto to Larry French for the Chastain article. Previous reviews I'd read somewhere didn't convince me to look him up. Three out of four of these articles are about newer and (to me at least) less well-known authors. See if you can keep this up. I welcome those on Old Masters or better-established authors, but especially appreciate those which introduce me to new talent. ¶ What did I miss? The *Saga*: should I keep on saying how much I enjoy it? I could, but I'd be repetitious. Surely you must know by now how much we Wolfe fans all appreciate it. When you are ready for book-form publication, if you can't interest a publisher, I'd be gald to help in any way I can at long distance. [*Several thanks, and I'll keep it in mind.*] Shibuk and Lachman: the former makes me wish we could get more, some, any, of the excellent British TV crime shows here in Pensacola. Mobil Oil promised a commercial TV presentation of James Mitchell's Callan series, but if it ever materialized it didn't make it here. I enjoyed the old *Avengers* and *Champions*, and even a couple of episodes of *Dr. Who* which I think were run by mistake. The latter makes me, like Jeff Banks, mildly irked for not thinking of it. Well, I don't know what Jeff's excuse is but mine is pure trepedation; I don't think it was as effortless as it appears, or at least it wouldn't have been for me! Letters: I *am* verbose. I'll have to try to get on an issue-by-issue comment basis. I might still ramble on, but it might be a bit less obvious. A *definitive* article on Parker? I never promised *that*! Actually, I enjoy the books tremendously and am sitting here with crossed fingers that someone doesn't beat me to it. You're probably "sick unto death" about comments on typos, but in self-defense I have to say that I know *The Blackbird* is a Grofield novel, but my little + got lost in transcription. [*Cringe!*] My fault, I think, I should have used a simpler system of indicating those which I lacked and those which were not Parker stories. I agree with your decision not to stray from the genre, much as I've enjoyed historical novels in the past. I also agree with Bob Briney's statement on the need for more knowledge of European works of fiction, but I hope this won't extend to foreign language articles. [Δηατ ηαxε υοξ λοτ αλαινστ ͺοθειλν ωανλξαλε αθτιψωεσ?] My mystery and detective reading is done first of all for pleasure and my very limited ability to read foreign languages would make such articles more an effort than an enjoyment. Finally, I'm sorry Ellen Nehr corrected that typo; I enjoyed the image conjured up by "comic" books. ¶ TMF 2:5 (Are you wondering where this burst of typewritten logorrhea has sprung from? My centipede lawn has finally, I hope, gone dormant and I no longer feel it will overwhelm the house if I don't beat it back once a week!) The Editorial: I think

you've said it for all of us; don't lose Steve Lewis! My
only complaint is that my "want to read" list is exceeding
my ability to keep ahead of. Incidentally, not only is Steve
an excellent reviewer, he puts out a nice book list. Lachman: I hope Marv will get back to the non-fiction "about"
crime reviews. These titles are usually the most expensive
and I like to see a few reviews before I buy! Kelley: (I
have a feeling I've been spelling George's name at times
with and without the final "e". Sorry, George, but you
should see what they do to mine!) He, like Wooster, doesn't
hesitate to call a clunker when he's read one, and we don't
always agree, but on Pronzini we do. I haven't read *A Run
in Diamonds* or *Games*, but I'm going to definitely get the
former because I want to see why George likens Carmody to
Parker. Parker as organizer, yes; as broker, no, unless I've
misunderstood what George meant by the term. I read the two
Dan Connell titles and had forgotten them until this article.
Bleiler: this is the excellent kind of article on non-English/American mystery writing we simple mono-lingual types
can appreciate, and it nicely complements Hedman's letter,
or vice-versa if you prefer. Wooster: this is a particularly
timely example of why I'm willing to accept Martin's occasional brutal forthrightness. (The transposition of pages
10 and 11 didn't register immediately. I thought that only a
few words between "to" and "have" had been dropped, which
only shows that I haven't read my volume yet!) Townsend:
Your comments on the dating of "Christmas Party" made me curious enough to check Archie's remark that he will "get a
raise the first of the year, which is a week from Monday."
Taking this to mean that January 1 will fall on a Monday, the
events of "Christmas Party" would have to take place in 1950
or 1961, according to the Perpetual Calendar in my *Official
Associated Press Almanac* of 1974. (You can see how up-to-date my home reference shelf is!) Was Archie (Stout) trying
to conceal the actual year in which this adventure took
place? Did Archie mean "a week from Monday" beginning with
the day *following* Monday, which could explain Baring-Gould's
placing the case in 1957, when January 1 fell on a *Tuesday*?
(I can see how the Sherlockians get tangled up in these internal inconsistencies!) Banks and Dawson: I think I'm undecided about chart articles. They do provide a great deal
of information in a limited space, but I like the more leisurely analysis of a good narrative article also. The introduction to this one was excellent. I have yet to read *The
Honourable Schoolboy*, but if Le Carré's latest is as definitive and final as Banks and Dawson judge it to be, I can only
hope he agrees. Too many authors reach a logical conclusion
in a series but can't resist a popular demand for "one more".
(I don't mean that all such "return" efforts are failures,
but many are.) Lewis, et al: about Steve, I've said it. (If
you can remember the dim, far-off beginnings of this seemingly endless missive.) The other reviews were also particularly good this time, or at least I thought so. "Documents":
welcome to Don Moskowitz from my old home town. Don, if we
get up next summer, as we usually do to visit relatives, I'll
give you a call. Other than the fact that we both want TAD
1-9, you sound like a nice guy! Michael Doran ruined my day
with his note on the probably demise of a Nero Wolfe series
along with the demise of Thayer David. Jeff Banks wondered
why none of the reviews of *Murder Ink* has listed all of the
contributors. Probably because there are 126 of them! As an

appreciation of Jeff's fine efforts in TMF (including his letters!), I've typed up a list from the "Contents" page, omitting repeats of the same name but not trying to sort out pseudonyms. I'm enclosing same. If you don't think there would be enough general interest to print it (or don't have the stamina to type it; I know how you feel about lists), send it on to Jeff with my compliments. I'll be glad to make a copy for anyone else who wants one if they'll send a SASE along with their request. [*I'll try to squeeze it in somewhere, but it's going to be a tight fit.*] Jeff also questions Amnon Kabatchnik's coupling of Archer and McGee in his reviews, which also bothered me a bit. I questioned Kabatchnik's referring to Quiller as a "double agent" in an earlier review, and I sincerely hope that he doesn't consider McGee to be a private eye. Perhaps he hasn't read all of the McGee series, for I could see his being misled by McGee's reasons for traveling north in *One Fearful Yellow Eye*. MacDonald has blurred the lines a bit since *The Deep Blue Good-by*, although I'm now not sure that I agree with Jeff that McGee is at his most "eye-like" in that one. Hum . . . more on that some other time. Martin Morse Wooster (this should have been included at the beginning, probably) is more intrepid that I would be in repeating conversations, unless he carries a concealed tape recorder, but they do make interesting reading. Seriously, though, I do hope that neither Martin nor any of the rest of us make any unsubstantiated statements which result in the pages of TMF being consumed with interminable rebuttals and counter-rebuttals (if there are such things). Here, Guy, I would hope that most of us would allow you to exercise your editorial judgement in cutting off public exchanges and refer the protagonists to each other. Thanks to Jeff Meyerson for the additional Parker information. I have gotten more from others and think I can fill in some of his blanks on dates and PB nos. but I'll wait until I do the article. So Iwan Hedman reads TMF in "about an hour", and English isn't even his native language! I haven't timed an issue yet, but I'm going to do so with 2:6; I know it takes me longer than that, at least if I'm going to recall the contents as well as he does. I'm glad to see that Steve Stillwell has another vote for his suggested article on collecting. (I met Steve at Bouchercon 9 and he told me then that mine was, so far, the only encouraging comment he had received.) I'll accept, and respect, Patricia Parnell's reasons for disliking spy fiction even if I disagree with them, but she shouldn't then proceed to comment on the sub-genre she is obviously unfamiliar with. Like him or not, Matt Helm has nothing--from a professional viewpoint--in common with those to whom she likens him. Most importantly, they were all losers; Matt isn't. I'm going to stick my neck out and say that I think a lot of people are fed up with, revolted by, frightened of, what have you, the *real* violence in the *real* world; violence they can neither ignore nor stop. Hence they turn away from it in the world of fiction, be it books, television or movies. That's fine; that's their personal decision and they are entitled to it *until* they take it a step further and decide that it should be censored so that *nobody* can read about it or see it. Then their arm has reached the end of my nose, and I object. How much further is it to deciding that personally objectionable concepts, acts, etc. should also be censored from the *real* news about the *real* world? As for the current myth that reading about or viewing violent acts encourages the commitment of same, see the article entitled "Is the TV Violence Issue a Red Herring?" by Irving D. Harris in the September 15, 1978 issue of *The Wall Street Journal*. ¶ Sorry, Guy--and others--I obviously feel strongly about this, but I'll try to restrain the hobby horse in the future. ¶ Since Patricia's letter was the last in 2:5, this is a good point to quit. [. . .]

CAST OF CONTRIBUTORS

From the Contents of *Murder Ink: The Mystery Reader's Companion*, perpetrated by Dilys Winn (New York: Workman, 1977). Compiled by David R. Doerrer.

For convenience in ascertaining the presence or absence of a particular name, the order of aypearance on the Contents pages has been changed to an alphabetical listing.

Abby Adams
Catherine Aird
Ted Allbeury
Frederick Arnold
Issac Asimov
Michael Baden
George Baker
Jacques Barzun
Gordon Bean
Washington C. Beenson
Edmund Bergler
Margaret Boe Birns
Peter Blake
K. Arne Blom
Stuart Bocher
John Boe
Carol Brener
Stanley H. Brown
Rosamund Bryce
Peter Bull
Heron Carvic
Ian Carmichael
Lionel Chelmsford
*Children's Express**
Paul Chevigny
Judith Crist
Hopley Croyden
Avon Curry
Eve Darge
Dorothy Salisbury Davis
William DeAndrea
Colin Dexter
Peter Dickinson
Hugh Douglas
Carolyn Fiske
Lee Fowler
Lawrence Frost
Herb Galewitz
John Gardner
Brian Garfield
Michael Gilbert
The Gordons

Harriet Grollier
Max Hall
Pete Hamill
Leonard R. Harris
Solomon Hastings
Laurence Henderson
Reginald Hill
Edward D. Hoch
Richard Hummler
P. D. James
Joan Kahn
H. R. F. Keating
Carol Kountz
Duncan Kyle
Vernon Lay
Jeanine Larmoth
Thomas Lask
John Leonard
Lowell J. Levine
Andrew B. Levy
Michael Z. Lewin
Abraham Lincoln
Richard R. Lingeman
Peter Lovesey
James McClure
Thomas M. McDade
Milt Machlin
Arnold Madison
Matthew J. Mahler
Eugene T. Maleska
Berkeley Mather
Gladys Mitchell
Carlotta Oglethorpe
Peter O'Donnell
James H. Olander
John P. Oliver
George O'Toole
Ione Paloma
Robert B. Parker
Kenneth Patchen
David Penn
Otto Penzler

R. J. Pilgrim
Joyce Porter
John L. Powers
Catherine Prezzano
Clifford A. Ridley
Donald Rumbelow
Christopher Rutledge
Violet St. Clair
Joyce Sanderson
Roy Scheider
Peter J. Schuyten
Hadrian Schwartz
Thomas Seligson
Ruth H. Smiley
Clyde Collins Snow
Joseph C. Stacey
Anthony Spiesman
Marilyn Stasio
Chris Steinbrunner
Ellen Stern
Lynn Strong
Eleanor Sullivan
Richard Townsend
Lawrence Treat
Alice K. Turner
Letitia Twyffert
Bill Vande Water
Peter N. Walker
Elizabeth Walter
Penelope Wallace
Colin Watson
John Watson
Warren Weith
Allison Wentworth
Donald E. Westlake
Phyllis A. Whitney
R. M. Whyte
Robin M. Winks
Dilys Winn
Rodger J. Winn
Anne Worboys
Margaret Yorke

* The name of the first newsmagazine written by children.

From Michael Cook, 3318 Wimberg Ave., Evansville, IN 47712: If you have space in the next issue would like very much to have the following inserted in the "unpaid advs": Wanted: Unicorn Mystery BC volume of four titles: McDougald-Woman Under the Mountain/Revell-The Silver Spade/Scherf-Curious Custard Pie/Ferrars-Hunt the Tortoise. . . .

From Viola Alice Sprenkle, 136 Landis Ave., Bridgeton, NJ 08302: In publishing this mystery letter, have you run across the new or most recent address for "The Sherlock Holmes Society of London"? I had been a member 6 years ago, and was planning to rejoin, if someone could provide me with the address. The last address I have is from a '72 publication, and that's outdated, I suppose. . . . If you don't know, could you provide an address of someone who does, or possibly an address of another Sherlock Holmes group? [*Can somebody out there help this lady?*]

From Carol Anderson, 233 Benham Road, Groton, CT 06340: I . . . have a request of you and possibly your readers. My students in chemistry for non-science majors have very little knowledge of laboratory work or a chemist in a working environment. I have found it useful to suggest novels, science fiction, and mysteries to broaden their knowledge of a scientist's work. Unfortunately, my bibliography of mysteries, such as *Whiff of Death*, is limited to a few books and short stories. Any suggestions would be most welcome.

Mary Ann Grochowski of Suspense Unlimited, 2009 So. 93rd St., West Allis, WI 53227, asks that everyone take note of her address change.

FLASH ---- DISREGARD ANY RUMORS YOU MAY HAVE HEARD TO THE EFFECT THAT DON MILLER HAS TAKEN ALL THE SUBSCRIPTION MONEYS FROM THE MYSTERY NOOK AND FLED TO RIO WHERE HE IS LIVING LIKE A KING. I HAVE SPOKEN TO HIM RECENTLY, IN WHEATON, AND HE ASSURES ME THAT THE NEXT NOOK WILL BE OUT BEFORE TOO MUCH LONGER. DON RUNS THE ONLY QUARTERLY IN THE BUSINESS THAT COMES OUT EVERY OTHER YEAR.

U.S. POSTAL SERVICE
STATEMENT OF OWNERSHIP, MANAGEMENT AND CIRCULATION
(Required by 39 U.S.C. 3685)

1. TITLE OF PUBLICATION: The MYSTERY FANcier
A. PUBLICATION NO.: 4 2 8 5 9 0
2. DATE OF FILING: 13 October 1978

3. FREQUENCY OF ISSUE: Bi-monthly
A. NO. OF ISSUES PUBLISHED ANNUALLY: 6
B. ANNUAL SUBSCRIPTION PRICE: $7.50

4. LOCATION OF KNOWN OFFICE OF PUBLICATION *(Street, City, County, State and ZIP Code) (Not printers)*
1120 Bluebird Lane, Memphis (Shelby County), TN 38116

5. LOCATION OF THE HEADQUARTERS OR GENERAL BUSINESS OFFICES OF THE PUBLISHERS *(Not printers)*
Same

6. NAMES AND COMPLETE ADDRESSES OF PUBLISHER, EDITOR, AND MANAGING EDITOR

PUBLISHER *(Name and Address)*
Guy M. Townsend, 1120 Bluebird Lane, Memphis, TN 38116

EDITOR *(Name and Address)*
Same

MANAGING EDITOR *(Name and Address)*
Same

7. OWNER *(If owned by a corporation, its name and address must be stated and also immediately thereunder the names and addresses of stockholders owning or holding 1 percent or more of total amount of stock. If not owned by a corporation, the names and addresses of the individual owners must be given. If owned by a partnership or other unincorporated firm, its name and address, as well as that of each individual must be given.)*

NAME	ADDRESS
Guy M. Townsend (Sole owner)	1120 Bluebird Lane, Memphis, TN 38116

8. KNOWN BONDHOLDERS, MORTGAGEES, AND OTHER SECURITY HOLDERS OWNING OR HOLDING 1 PERCENT OR MORE OF TOTAL AMOUNT OF BONDS, MORTGAGES OR OTHER SECURITIES *(If there are none, so state)*

NAME	ADDRESS
None	

9. FOR COMPLETION BY NONPROFIT ORGANIZATIONS AUTHORIZED TO MAIL AT SPECIAL RATES *(Section 132.122, PSM)*
The purpose, function, and nonprofit status of this organization and the exempt status for Federal income tax purposes *(Check one)*

☐ HAVE NOT CHANGED DURING PRECEDING 12 MONTHS ☐ HAVE CHANGED DURING PRECEDING 12 MONTHS
(If changed, publisher must submit explanation of change with this statement.)

10. EXTENT AND NATURE OF CIRCULATION	AVERAGE NO. COPIES EACH ISSUE DURING PRECEDING 12 MONTHS	ACTUAL NO. COPIES OF SINGLE ISSUE PUBLISHED NEAREST TO FILING DATE
A. TOTAL NO. COPIES PRINTED *(Net Press Run)*	300	300
B. PAID CIRCULATION		
1. SALES THROUGH DEALERS AND CARRIERS, STREET VENDORS AND COUNTER SALES	0	0
2. MAIL SUBSCRIPTIONS	150	150
C. TOTAL PAID CIRCULATION *(Sum of 10B1 and 10B2)*	150	150
D. FREE DISTRIBUTION BY MAIL, CARRIER OR OTHER MEANS SAMPLES, COMPLIMENTARY, AND OTHER FREE COPIES	12	13
E. TOTAL DISTRIBUTION *(Sum of C and D)*	162	163
F. COPIES NOT DISTRIBUTED		
1. OFFICE USE, LEFT OVER, UNACCOUNTED, SPOILED AFTER PRINTING	138	137
2. RETURNS FROM NEWS AGENTS	0	0
G. TOTAL *(Sum of E, F1 and 2—should equal net press run shown in A)*	300	300

11. I certify that the statements made by me above are correct and complete.

SIGNATURE AND TITLE OF EDITOR, PUBLISHER, BUSINESS MANAGER, OR OWNER
Guy M. Townsend, Editor

12. FOR COMPLETION BY PUBLISHERS MAILING AT THE REGULAR RATES *(Section 132.121, Postal Service Manual)*

39 U. S. C. 3626 provides in pertinent part: "No person who would have been entitled to mail matter under former section 4359 of this title shall mail such matter at the rates provided under this subsection unless he files annually with the Postal Service a written request for permission to mail matter at such rates."

In accordance with the provisions of this statute, I hereby request permission to mail the publication named in item 1 at the phased postage rates presently authorized by 39 U. S. C. 3626.

SIGNATURE AND TITLE OF EDITOR, PUBLISHER, BUSINESS MANAGER, OR OWNER
Guy M. Townsend, Editor

PS Form 3526, Mar. 1977 *(Page 1)* (See instructions on reverse)

www.ingramcontent.com/pod-product-compliance
Lightning Source LLC
Chambersburg PA
CBHW032217040426
42449CB00005B/636